THE
NEW
MEDIA
LITERACY
HANDBOOK

THE
NEW
MEDIA
LITERACY
HANDBOOK

AN EDUCATOR'S GUIDE
TO BRINGING NEW MEDIA
INTO THE CLASSROOM

CORNELIA BRUNNER, PH.D.
AND WILLIAM TALLY

ANCHOR BOOKS
DOUBLEDAY
New York London Toronto Sydney Auckland

AN ANCHOR BOOK
PUBLISHED BY DOUBLEDAY
a division of Random House, Inc.
1540 Broadway, New York, New York 10036

ANCHOR BOOKS, DOUBLEDAY, and the portrayal of an anchor are trademarks of Doubleday, a division of Random House, Inc.

Library of Congress Cataloging-in-Publication Data

Brunner, Cornelia, Ph.D.
    The new media literacy handbook: an educator's guide to bringing new media into the classroom / Cornelia Brunner & William Tally.
      p. cm.
    Includes index.
    1. Educational technology—Handbooks, manuals, etc. 2. Media literacy—Handbooks, manuals, etc. 3. Interactive multimedia—Handbooks, manuals, etc. 4. Computer-assisted instruction—Handbooks, manuals, etc. I. Tally, William. II. Title.
LB1028.3.B77 1999
371.33'4—dc21
                           99-11339
                           CIP

Text design by Stanley S. Drate / Folio Graphics Co. Inc.

10 9 8 7 6 5 4 3 2 1

◆ Acknowledgments ◆

First and foremost the authors wish to thank the Bertelsmann Foundation for supporting the Media Workshop New York, the program of curriculum development, teacher training, and research out of which this book emerged. It is not every day that a global media conglomerate chooses to help urban schoolteachers make their students more critical, creative, and discerning about the media they consume and the technologies they use. We were lucky, in particular, to work with Dr. Ingrid Hamm from the Foundation, who recognized the need for this work from the beginning and helped shape it throughout. We also owe heartfelt thanks to our friend Melissa Phillips, director of the Media Workshop, and all her staff, who helped us refine these ideas through practical work with teachers, and taught us much in the process. The best of the thinking in this book grows, however, from more than ten years of arguments, explorations, and conversations with our colleagues at the EDC Center for Children and Technology, who have never failed to be challenging and stimulating and supportive, even when we didn't deserve it. Weaknesses of the writing are all ours, since we benefited from the care and attention of our talented editor and close friend, Lorin Driggs. Finally the authors offer our greatest thanks, as well as a standing plea for forgiveness for putting up with us, to our respective partners in love and life, Lucy Gilbert and Peggy Tally.

This book is dedicated to Jan Hawkins, 1952–1999.

◆ Contents ◆

· 1 ·

Introduction

❖

❖ **Why This Book?**

This book grows out of the work of the Media Workshop New York (MWNY), a professional development program for teachers in New York City. The mission of MWNY is to "help teachers support their classroom practice through the critical use of media and technology." The work that teachers do at MWNY is grounded in the belief that media and technology are tools; that the successful integration of these tools into any classroom requires, as the essential minimum, professional support for teachers; and that adequate professional support for teachers must include preparing them to take a critical view of the design, content, and use of these new learning tools in relation to the curriculum and its specific learning goals and in relation to teaching practice.

The purpose of this book is to show the many ways new media and technologies work well as tools for good teaching and learning and to provide a framework for the critical analysis of these tools. The particular vision of what constitutes "good teaching and learning" in the minds of the authors is discussed fully in the next chapter. First, however, we will describe some of the practical uses for new technologies and media in classrooms, and then we will delve into media literacy as an essential part of the equation.

◆ Roles for Technologies in Schools

The chapters that follow discuss many specific roles for new media as they relate to disciplinary goals in language arts, science, social studies, and art. In this section we will characterize three general ways that technologies can support democratic learning in information-age schools: as tools for student research, as tools for student production, and as tools for public conversations.

As research tools, new media can support the values and habits of inquiry-learning. As production tools, new media can support students in shaping meaning out of their experiences, expressing meaning in different forms and languages, reflecting on and assessing the value of their work, and sharing it with different audiences. As conversational tools, new media can link students in dialogue with peers and adults in and beyond the school, and promote the democratic value of communication and mutual understanding in a diverse society. Taken together, this way of viewing educational work—as cycles of student-directed research, production, and conversation—creates a school culture in which continuous inquiry and reflection are the norm. The following discussion of each category of new media tools offers examples of technology genres in that category.

Tools for Student Research

Research tools, broadly conceived, include any new media applications that support the inquiry process. The inquiry approach to teaching gives students wide latitude in shaping their investigations, from posing questions of interest and concern to them, to locating and analyzing resources, to revising questions and hypotheses and synthesizing findings. Yet students need guidance and support in this process. New technology applications can help by a) posing complex "cases" that engage students and invite questions; b) giving students access to rich and timely content materials; c) enabling students to record and measure real-world, real-time data; and d) guiding students in analyzing, interpreting, contextualizing, and making sense of their findings and summarizing and synthesizing them as well.

Examples of media applications that support these phases of

the inquiry process abound. Computer-based simulations create ideal environments for generating authentic student questions. So do on-line encounters with real-world activities such as scientific expeditions, which classrooms can increasingly join for extended or short-term periods. The *Passport to Knowledge* program (passport.ivv.nasa.gov/) and the popular Quest series projects with Dan Buettner's expedition team (www.classroom.com/onlinecatalog/34.asp) enable students to join real scientists as they explore the planet Mars and the ancient cultures of the earth respectively, and both demonstrate that students' questions are often as valid and worthwhile as those of scientists.

The World Wide Web, with its global reach and its increasingly deep and varied digital libraries, is an obvious example of a research tool giving access to rich and timely material. CD-ROM "encyclopedias," including databases of art, culture, history, science topics, and other areas, are also ubiquitous, and can be used to advantage for student research. But media literacy skills must be applied with these as with all media, especially when doing research, since the quality and form of the material on the Web and CD-ROMs vary greatly, to say the least. At the most basic level, the evolving search capabilities of most school library electronic indexes are important research tools that students need to learn to navigate, as they can enable students to get more, and more appropriate source materials on their own than ever before. Here again skill in evaluating the results of searches is essential for students to develop.

Students can also use media tools to observe, record, and analyze real-time phenomena, both natural and social. Microcomputer-based laboratories, or MBLs, attach electronic probes to classroom computers and turn them into instruments for measuring and graphing many different kinds of physical data, including temperature, pressure, sound, and light. In a less high-tech vein, a simple video camcorder can be used to capture fleeting or long-term patterns in physical or social phenomena for study. For example, students can shoot and replay in slow motion science experiments that are over in only seconds in order to better analyze the data; or they can record and analyze the movements of people through hallways and in courtyards to study ways that environmental design affects social interactions. Used in the documentary genre, video also enables students to go beyond the confines of their school and into their local community, to interview old people, youth, civic leaders, and ordinary people about issues of importance to them. As always, students and teachers must keep in mind the properties of the media they use to record and "document" reality, the ways they limit the aspects of the world that are captured, and the aspects of the world they leave out.

Less common are media tools that support students in analyzing, interpreting, contextualizing, and making sense of their findings and summarizing and synthesizing them as well. In general, this phase of the inquiry process requires the work of a good teacher more than a machine. However there are two kinds of computer-based programs that fit this category. First, there are "tool" applications such as spreadsheets, databases, and image-processing programs that enable students to manipulate data in order to find emergent patterns in it. Second, there are programs that "outline" the research process for students, and these may prompt them to assess a source's authorship, point of view, main argument, supporting evidence, relevance to the research question, etc. In the future, look for Web-based tools that offer critical and analytic "frames" that automatically surround material that users navigate to, prompting them to analyze and evaluate the contents.

Tools for Student Production

In the information-age school, student work often finds tangible expression in a product that can be shared with multiple audiences, not just with the teacher. Production tools, broadly considered, include any technology applications that enable students to shape and express the meaning of what they are learning in forms that can be shared with others. A key advantage of this teaching approach is that students' products can be "exported" from the classroom and school, to find meaning and value in other places and with other constituencies. Here they can serve as the focus of reflection and conversation about the criteria of a good performance or product as well as a good education. This process can open educational discourse up to more people—including other educators, community members, and experts—enabling the building of a democratic consensus on the meaning and value of educational practices that will almost certainly fail without such consensus.

Media-based production aids now include Web-based authoring and publishing tools; multimedia and hypertext tools for creating and annotating reports, newspapers, and nonlinear documents; graphics and animation programs for rendering layered visual representations and even movies; and camcorders and video editors and animators that enable students to create their own dramatic and documentary videos. Each of these media has its own formal features or "language," its own potential audiences, and its own strengths and limitations as a medium of student expression.

Teachers encouraging students to become authors in a given medium need to take into account the challenges of learning the medium's language, the suitability of the medium to the material, and whether the resulting product will find an appropriate audience beyond the classroom. The organization of classroom work must also be taken into account. Some media, such as video, are highly collaborative in nature. Others, such as hypertext, are less so. As with any effort to master a new medium, students need time and opportunities to create multiple "drafts"—and have them warmly but critically reviewed—in order to be successful. In general, the "writing process" model of authorship is a good one to apply to any form of student creativity: students should be given opportunities to brainstorm ideas important to them, "freewrite" to explore the ideas, create several drafts in which meaning is both focused and elaborated, and receive feedback from peers and adults.

The rewards of student production can be great. Take video production, for example. At the Educational Video Center in New York City, high-school-age students from around the city collaborate to create independent documentary videos on topics of importance to them, including racial stereotypes, music, AIDS awareness, the culture of rap, unequal schooling, the possibility of life after high school, and police-youth relations. Working in teams, the teenagers brainstorm, research, write, shoot, edit, and present a broadcast-quality documentary, screening it before audiences of peers, family members, and community members. All the while, they build portfolios containing the phone research they do, the interview questions they create, their logs of video shot, and their rough and final cuts of the video. At the end of each term, panels of teachers, media makers, and community members assess the portfolios in roundtable sessions based on public criteria and give the student producers careful feedback on their performance. Ultimately, accompanied by teacher guides, the students' videotapes become curriculum materials distributed to schools and community centers nationally and are sometimes broadcast on major network television.

Media production by EVC high school students demonstrates that schools—and, more important, children—can be *contributors* to the society and culture around them, not simply *recipients* of what the larger culture has decided are the appropriate ideas and skills for them to acquire. Student contributions in many areas of endeavor—scientific investigations, cultural translation, social ethnography—can potentially be of great value, but in the area of public culture they are crucial. In our media-saturated world the voices and perspectives of many people—young people included—are routinely elided. Because of this, student video production around social issues has the potential to correct some of the biases and contradictions inherent in a corporate-owned "public" sphere. Students at EVC are not simply studying and critiquing the messages and forms of mass media—they are actively *changing* the media that people see and use by adding their own unique views and voices as urban minority youth. All students' views matter, and are needed somewhere. High school students in Appalachia working with the Appalshop video collective are likewise challenging and changing mass media portrayals of rural culture with their own cultural journalism.

Student production in the newer media—hypertext, multimedia, on the Web—must be undertaken with an awareness of the unique strengths and limitations of these media. In a hypertext or hypermedia document, what does the nonlinear nature of the text enable students to say or do differently with the material, and what purposes does this feature serve? How can students be helped to explore and understand this capability, as both authors and readers? These are particularly important questions to address because there are as of yet no clear standards or conventions guiding our use of nonlinear texts, nor the purposes to which we put them. These and related issues of "reality," authorship, and ownership that arise when students produce "new" works using media tools and incorporating content that becomes accessible and changeable using new technologies are discussed elsewhere in this book. In all of their conversations with students as these questions arise in the classroom, it is important for teachers to cultivate and reinforce repeatedly the media literacy habits of mind outlined below.

Tools for Public Conversations

With the growth of network technologies like the Internet, computers in school no longer function simply as storage or computational media but are being broadly reconceived as communications media. The familiar desktop "box" was first transformed into a "pipeline" for the delivery of rich material and is now beginning to function as a "node" in a vast network of communications. The implications of this shift on education are not yet clear, but in theory, schools stand to benefit greatly. After all, schools are one of the few remaining institutions in which professionals cannot count on access to the most basic communications technology, the telephone, and in which teachers and students routinely complain of isolation from the outside world. From this perspective, wiring classrooms—connecting existing computers to a network—holds the possibility of forging connections between students, teachers, and the world beyond the classroom.

Like all technology-related transformations, however, this one will happen only if accompanied by many other changes in school organization and culture. Schools need to be wired humanly even more than they need to be wired electronically; that is, schools need to be supported by better, more informed, and more trusting relationships between parents, teachers, students, administrators, and community members. Technologies can help create the conditions for these relationships and these conversations to happen; but a school's rules, norms, and values—especially those around who gets to speak, to whom, and for what purposes—are the more important preconditions.

What are public conversations, and why are they important

in the democratic, information-age school? What technologies exist to support them?

By public conversations we mean reflective exchanges about the meaning and value of the information and knowledge being built in school. The conversations could be between students at the classroom level, between teachers and parents at the school-household level, or between school members and a far-flung community. When students sit in a circle and discuss their different views of current events, this is a public conversation; when they interview a local official about waste disposal, this is a public conversation; when parents help evaluate student portfolios and share their ideas about student work, this is a public conversation. Likewise, when a student struggling to make sense of Shakespeare logs onto a Web site to post a question about *Macbeth* and receives replies from a graduate student, a professor of English literature, and an actor, this is a public conversation; when teachers working toward professional development talk about their teaching practices with other teachers on-line, this is a public conversation; when parents log on to a school's Web site and comment on curriculum, or students pose questions to scientists debating the effects of global warming, these are public conversations. These kinds of exchanges can be supported by a variety of technologies—e-mail at the most basic, real-time Web chats and distance learning configurations at a more technically advanced level, and threaded conferencing systems, bulletin boards, and list servs at an intermediate level.

Public conversations are common in the democratic information-age school for two main reasons. First, it is through such conversations that thinking becomes manifest, that reflective and critical habits of mind become routine. Where facts are not worshipped for their own sake, but are respected instead for their power or weight in grounding arguments, the arguments themselves must happen everywhere, all the time. Second, conversations are common because through them students learn democratic habits that are crucial in a pluralistic school and a pluralistic society in which people are allowed to come to very different conclusions about the world. Learning to listen to and respect arguments that are different from your own, and make yourself understood by others who do not agree with you, and forge consensus around shared ideas and values are crucial skills in our democratic society.

It should be noted that a crucial precondition for public conversations to happen is trust: trust for students, and trust for teachers. Free communication always poses risks to the established rules and norms, as every dictator, but also every democratic leader knows. Currently many schools are nervous about giving students the freedom to use e-mail, for example, fearing it might be abused either by students or by others seeking to harm them. And indeed, in any school where students have been given their own e-mail accounts and the ability to post to school bulletin boards or list servs, childish abuses and excesses—such as "flaming" or derogatory speech—have generally occurred. Yet we know of schools where this kind of incident has led to a school-wide dialogue about the kind of community that students want and the kinds of speech and forms of address that are compatible with it. In one school, a whole-school meeting led students to brainstorm a list of "guidelines" for speech in hallways and on-line. The refining of this list—including debates about rules that were overbroad or too restrictive—continued on-line until the school community had a series of guidelines it could live with. In this instance, at least, the presence of a communications technology served as a catalyst, as well as a vehicle, of democratic debate and discussion.

◆ A New, Compelling Need for Media Literacy

As teachers increasingly integrate the new media into their curricula, they need to invent a set of working criteria to evaluate commercial media products for use by their students and to assess the media productions of their own students in a developmentally appropriate fashion. Yet few teachers have been provided with much opportunity to develop a language, a set of useful concepts, with which to think critically about the form as well as the content of these new multimedia texts. They can judge the quality of the content of a video or a CD-ROM or a Web site, but not the quality of its structure. All of us learned in school how to analyze a range of written texts, from poems to research reports. Most teachers can explain why they consider a particular piece of writing polemical rather than neutral, for instance. They can point to the fact, for example, that an assertion in an opening sentence is not followed by some kind of substantiation in the rest of the paragraph as an instance of its polemical nature. Yet few have this kind of structural understanding of images and sounds, and of multimedia texts. They may recognize the difference between a polemical and a neutral image as easily as a media expert, but they do not necessarily have the words, the tool kit of media concepts, with which to explain their understanding.

Being media literate, however, means not only knowing when and how to use these new media, but also being able to understand both their content and their structure. It means having some basic understanding of how media are constructed, how they are distributed, who owns them, and how they express the values and the perspective of their authors in the way they are made as well as in what they cover. It is our hope that this book might aid teachers in integrating some important media literacy concepts into the curriculum along with the media themselves. By adding a short but powerful, critical look at the medium being used in a lesson, teachers can develop evaluative criteria for and with their students anywhere in the curriculum without having to make the media a separate subject of study. Some of the special challenges posed by new media and technologies are described below.

What's Real?

New technologies make it possible to edit, alter, combine, and otherwise manipulate images, blurring the distinctions between "authentic" and "fake." Here's a case in point:

> A group of students wants to illustrate what cowboys wore during the opening of the western frontier. They look at many images, but no single one captures all the articles of clothing they think are significant. Using an electronic paint program, they take parts of different images, the head with a hat from one, the chest with a shirt and vest from another, and so on, and compose a whole, perfectly dressed cowboy. They are particularly proud of themselves for finding a picture of a cowboy boot in an old clothing catalogue. There

is only one left boot, but they copy and flip it and put a beautiful, identical one on their composite cowboy's foot. They are pleased with themselves because in almost all the full pictures of cowboys they found, the boots are hidden by trousers and chaps. In their presentation to the class, they see no reason to mention the fact that this image is a composite. To their way of thinking, if each part of a composite image is "real," that is, a photograph of a genuine historical object or person rather than a "fake" computer-generated rendering, the composite image represents a reality as well.

What Is the Message?

Because they are image- and/or sound-rich and engaging, new technologies may seem to speak for themselves, when, in fact, the meaning is often provided by the viewer's particular point of view and personal biases, losing the intended message. For example:

An eighth-grader's history project consists of compiling a set of video clips depicting the treatment of women in Hollywood movies about the western frontier. She works very hard to find and edit a tape of relevant clips. In her presentation to the class, she shows each clip and then talks about the way it exemplifies a particular set of assumptions about the role of women and contrasts it with the reality of women's lives on the frontier. She has done a great deal of excellent research, but her presentation falls flat because she fails to realize that everybody does not see the same thing when they look at a video clip. Nobody has taught her to call her audience's attention to the things she wants them to see. When her fellow students do not see the stereotyping that seems so blatant to her, she feels discouraged and a little betrayed by her peers. She thinks they don't understand what she is trying to say about sexism. Her teacher, who knows what she was trying to say, of course, praises her presentation and gives her the good grade she deserves, but misses an opportunity for visual literacy education by not asking her to show a clip again—after framing it with her analysis. Had she done so, the other students in the class might have had an opportunity to experience the difference in their own reading of the clip, thereby making concrete the concept of point of view in film which the student was trying to demonstrate in her presentation.

What's Important?

New technologies may lead to inadvertent or unintentional messages, emphases, or interpretations that distort the purpose or meaning of the information. Here's an example:

> A group of teachers are analyzing the performance of a fellow teacher by looking at a videotape. They make a number of positive comments while the tape shows the young teacher at the board, explaining a complex concept. They think he is doing a fine job explaining things. Suddenly, the camera pulls back to reveal a close-up of a student resting his head on a desk in the foreground with the teacher pointing to the blackboard in the background. At this point the group's perception of the teacher's performance changes dramatically. They start to focus more on the fact that the teacher is talking at the students rather than interacting with them. Their discussion now focuses away from the content of what he is saying and more on the relationship between the teacher and the students. They do not ask themselves whether this one student they happened to see on camera is representative of the entire class. Without realizing it, they treat this piece of video documentation as if it were a documentary: They assume that the shot of the student was included because it represents an important aspect of the truth. In fact, the shot was the result of the camera operator, an untrained research assistant, moving the camera momentarily to make room for a student passing by. None of the teachers discussing the tape realize the extent to which their perceptions are influenced by media conventions. They believe they are evaluating the teacher's performance rather than a representation of his performance.

◆ Aspects of Media Literacy

Using media appropriately requires understanding their strengths as well as their limitations. As teachers approach this new world of digital media, they find themselves in a position—usually without adequate preparation—to cope with a number of complex issues:

- ◆ Understanding even the customary criteria for evaluating the value and relevance of traditional media productions is becoming more critical as raw, unedited, unsolicited information enters the classroom via the Internet. Teachers who have been able to rely on publishers, editors, curriculum directors, and master teachers to select appropriate materials for them can still do so, but the degree of control they have over what information their "wired" students are exposed to is seriously curtailed. Now they need new criteria and useful strategies to help these students make positive and constructive use of that information.

♦ As more multimedia products appear, both in CD-ROM format and on the Web, *visual literacy,* a deeper understanding of visual representation, becomes increasingly important as more of the material is visual in nature. In addition to the need for understanding how images convey meaning, teachers and students have to be prepared to understand how the mix of media—text, image, effect, and sound—interrelate.

♦ The *nonlinear* organization of these new media presents teachers with a demand to teach students how to interpret and construct meanings in a medium that is not only brand new (and thus in an experimental stage with no clear guidelines or customs to rely on) but also represents, at least potentially, a genuine shift in the way we think about representing knowledge and thus requires a new set of interpretive and authoring skills to be learned by students and teachers at the same time.

Let us look at these issues one at a time.

Evaluation Criteria

There is much talk everywhere in the educational community about the information explosion, about being left out or being inundated. Some people compare the Internet to untreated sewage, others consider it a fountain of knowledge. In either case, there is agreement that we can shelter students only a short while before we have to let them go out there into the information jungle and cope with what they encounter. Standards, criteria, guidelines—the notion that students need a set of working concepts to help them distinguish the wheat from the chaff, to find what they need and to navigate between misinformation and free expression, and to make appropriate and constructive use of these newly available resources, is a paramount concern for most educators responsible for integrating technology into their schools. Teachers can certainly tell whether something is relevant to their curriculum and developmentally suitable for their students, but they need help locating, editing, and collecting relevant information even if it comes right into their classroom.

On-line services that find, evaluate, contextualize, and describe relevant digital resources may be becoming the textbook editors of the future. But right now there is no friendly, helpful librarian between the students and the information they encounter in the course of their on-line research. Teachers and librarians, or media specialists, can guide their searches, but there are no longer any locked cases with material considered unsuitable for general consumption. Parents are going to get upset. Kids are going to get confused and misinformed. The only choice we have is to provide our children and their teachers with opportunities to discuss these issues, to invent and experiment with a set of criteria that work to tag questionable content, leaving it up to the information consumers to apply a set of strategies for checking out information, much like a good journalist does. The structure of the presentation, assumptions about the audience, values embedded in the form as well as the content, are crucially important elements in the tool kit of critical concepts brought to bear on new information.

New criteria are important not only for evaluating information produced by others but also for assessing student work. Multimedia tools give students the ability to recontextualize, alter, and animate information. This can lead to many interesting explorations of what kind of information is best captured or expressed through what medium. Too often, students spend a great deal of time focusing on the wrong thing. For instance, an eighth-grade student project about the expansion of the American frontier, a collaboratively produced hypertext document, had a relatively complex animation of a train blowing smoke and moving across the screen, followed by a single still image of a map showing the famous trails across the West. An animated map in which the trails come to life either geographically or historically would be far more informative, of course, but the students spent all the time they had available on the far less revealing animation of the train. The teacher admired the students' ingenuity— animation was something they had taught themselves—but never questioned its contribution to the project as a whole.

Visual Literacy

Visual literacy is not a new issue. Teachers who have taken courses in art, art history, or film have had some opportunities to become acquainted with the set of useful concepts that enables us to communicate about images in words. These courses are neither required, nor do they fit into the cramped program of most teachers during in-service teacher training. Scientists and historians have concepts to help them analyze evidence in a variety of forms, including visual evidence. In the literary world there are concepts about composition, tone, and rhythm comparable to their usage in the world of the visual arts. There are concepts, then, in every major school discipline for examining and thinking critically about visual representations. It is rare, however, that teachers in subjects other than art focus specific attention on the use of these concepts for interpreting, evaluating, and constructing visual representations.

A science teacher is far more likely to comment on the content of a graph produced by students than on its presentation, except if it is incorrect, misleading, or incomprehensible. Many science teachers consider it an important part of scientific literacy to be able to distinguish genuine scientific information from misleading graphic representations in the mass media, for instance, but rarely connect that concern to the way in which they teach their students to represent information. Often, there is a correct way, a form the student is supposed to follow, without much discussion of options and their meaning or of the origins of conventional ways of representing scientific findings. In history class, images are often used as illustrations rather than as evidence. The historical tools that are used to investigate images as primary sources, to distinguish between observing and cataloguing the content of a photograph, for instance, and interpreting it, are rarely explicitly taught. History teachers often talk about how an image "shows us" what happened without examining explicitly what images can and cannot show. They do not necessarily convey the importance of forensic concepts to counteract our tendency to make sense of an ambiguous image by connecting its elements through a plausible story, in other words, and assuming that an image contains a narrative rather than realizing that we invented it.

Teachers need a way to connect rigorous concepts about evidence in science and history with the power of the ideas about how images evoke meanings in the humanities. Visual literacy, as a major component of media education, is a possible unifying concept. Many of the activities or lesson ideas presented in this book will thus focus on visual literacy, on more systematic ways of examining the visual structure as well as on the content of the wealth of images now available in the classroom.

Hypermedia

The combination of multiple media, including sounds and moving images, requires additional emphasis on visual literacy, but it does not present teachers with an entirely new set of skills to consider. The mix of media has been around for a while, since the introduction of the film strip—but now there is so much more of this kind of information in every domain. What is truly new, however, is the interactive nature of this medium, and its nonlinear organization. We do not yet understand the implications of this nonlinearity. As with every new medium, we initially import texts from older media while we try to understand first what added value the new medium brings, and then start to experiment with new kinds of texts made possible by the medium itself.

In the case of this new medium, hypertext, which gives the reader the ability to interact with the text, to decide the scope and sequence of the information rather than follow the author on a predetermined path, has implications for both readers and authors. Readers are, perhaps, most familiar with this kind of organization of information from encyclopedias and dictionaries. We do not assume a "dear reader" in an encyclopedia, someone who follows the argument carefully and to whom the author can explain things as they become salient to the argument of the text. Encyclopedia entries are designed to stand alone. We are not expected to read the entries under the letter B before going on to the letter C. Encyclopedia entries need a particular kind of integrity. They have to include enough introductory information to provide a context for the more specific description of the phenomenon under discussion, do so for a variety of readers with a range of expertise, and do so in as succinct a manner as possible. They also usually provide some links to related information. The links can be in the form of pointers to other entries or to books and resources on which the entry is based. In the case of dictionary entries, links can take the form of synonyms or opposites. It is assumed that some readers will want to follow those links to find out more about a topic, while others will ignore them and either be satisfied with the amount of information they found or make links of their own by finding relevant information elsewhere, based, however, on their new understanding of the topic. This is the essence of hypertext.

We need a good metaphor for what the nonlinear structure provides by way of opportunity for new forms of expression and new ways of distributing and gathering information. In a hypertext document, a range of possibilities is offered to the reader, tied together conceptually by some theme or metaphor. Readers choose their own path through the material, depending on their needs and interests. In many ways, good multimedia hypertext is like a well-stocked, open, student-centered classroom with inviting learning centers scattered about, plenty of interesting-looking resources on shelves and in cupboards, and examples of student work everywhere. In a well-designed classroom, these opportunities for learning are tied together through a theme—the topic students are researching, debating with each other, and discussing with their teacher. Teachers who know how to design this kind of learning environment understand something about the central design issues in multimedia hypertext development: how to provide enough guidance and framework to make it possible for students to discover things on their own without getting lost but without being too directive and controlling so much of the process that students end up following along a predetermined path rather than constructing their own. In such a classroom, every child does not learn the same things. Students follow their own interests within a set of parameters supplied by the teacher and share the knowledge they gather in their investigations with each other.

In that sense, some teachers are quite familiar with this new medium. In another sense, however, this medium is quite different from any other kind of writing and requires that we teach students special authoring and design skills. One of the most important differences between linear and nonlinear media is that the author has to provide multiple links between different parts of the information. Organizing information into related clusters and describing how the various clusters are linked is one of the writing skills needed for nonlinear authoring. Perhaps the most powerful educational aspect of nonlinear texts is this capacity to link diverse ideas to each other for a variety of reasons, thus providing multiple entry or focal points for different audiences. All too often, however, this is the part that's left out when students start to use hypertext.

A group of students may be doing research on a topic, like the opening of the West, for example. Each student (or small group) will collect information and prepare a few cards or pages of findings, some about the railroads, some about Native Americans, etc. Each contribution will probably contain some text, some images, maybe an animation or a video clip, and perhaps some sound clips. They will be strung together through the table of contents, which will contain links that lead to each theme or subtopic. Together they will make quite a rich report on the overall topic, in a kind of hub-and-spokes structure, where each "chapter" is self-contained, and can usually be navigated through in a linear fashion (or contain its own internal hub-and-spokes substructure with linear subchapters). Navigation is within the chapter and there are links on every page to go to the next page, the previous page, and back to the table of contents.

The missed opportunity, typically, lies in failing to create the conceptual links between the ideas included within the chapters. Ideally, students would finish their contributions, examine the whole project report, discuss how ideas within each of their chapters relate to each other—and then create those links and annotate them (i.e., describe how they see the ideas relating to each other). That would be using what is new about this medium: that it allows the associations among ideas across sections of the content. This is also the greatest educational promise of the medium: that students discuss how their findings and interpretations relate to each other rather than assuming that the teacher is the only real audience for their work. Many teachers want this process to happen but find that the project takes far longer than they planned and so there is no time left for this final reflective discussion and linking of related ideas. There might be a kind of summary discussion in which the teacher and students draw some conclusions about the topic across the various reports by students, but it is rarely the case that students get the opportunity to link their own work with that of others and thus see how different perspectives on the topic (represented by the various research foci of the different students) come up with different kinds of links. But it is precisely this kind of thinking about the relationship between ideas that most teachers consider important—and that they wish they had more opportunity to foster. The nonlinear nature of hypertext supports exactly that kind of connecting of ideas.

Five Critical Questions

One of the organizing principles or conceptual tools teachers can offer students is a set of critical questions they can learn to ask themselves about any medium they use. These kinds of questions can also be described as habits of mind—ways to approach any media experience, whether the media are traditional or new. Media educators have defined a range of such critical questions. The particular five critical questions we use at the Media Workshop New York can be summarized as follows:

How was this constructed?

However realistic, natural, or factual a media product may seem, it is never simply a "slice of life." It is always a construction. Rather than mirroring reality, it represents a specific aspect of reality from a particular perspective.

What values underlie this?

The media convey values both through the content they present and through the form these presentations take. Sometimes the values are explicit, sometimes they are hidden behind an apparently neutral stance, but they are always present, even if they are so much part of the shared assumptions of the mainstream culture that they do not need to be explicitly included.

What are the conventions used in this?

Media productions, new and old, are shaped by the acceptance of certain conventions users are expected to know. Media-literate consumers and producers must know these conventions and recognize their importance in shaping the way the media text is interpreted, whether they are adhered to or disregarded.

Who is the intended audience for this?

Each media text is intended for a particular audience. Recognizing not only what assumptions about the target audience are built into the text, but also how different audiences might interpret the same text, bringing their own assumptions, values, and conventions to it, is an important part of being able to evaluate a media production.

Who owns this? Who benefits from it?

Most media products are made for profit. Students may not have to understand the economics of media production and dissemination in great depth, but they should be aware that at least one purpose of many of the editorial and creative decisions made by producers has to do with selling something. It is thus important to consider who might be trying to sell what to whom when evaluating a media text.

◆ What This Book Offers

The following chapters are intended to offer a way of looking at the integration of media and technologies into classroom as an opportunity to improve teaching and learning and to address the critical media literacy issues that go hand in hand with them.

Chapter 2 places media and technologies within a pedagogical context—a particular view of teaching and learning—and leads ultimately to the place these new tools have in the school reform movement.

Chapters 3 through 6 are discipline-specific, examining media and technologies in the context of the real demands and opportunities of the history, art, English/language arts, and science curriculum. Included in each of these chapters is a discussion of content standards, examples of ways new media and technology applications can serve student learning and teaching practice, and related media literacy issues.

While the authors worked collaboratively on the entire book, and especially the introduction, Brunner took primary responsibility for writing chapters 4 and 5, and Tally for chapters 2, 3, and 6.

2

Technology for Change:
A NEW VISION OF TEACHING
AND LEARNING

Introduction

The chief premise behind this book is that media and technologies are tools. They are not, in other words, ends in themselves. They may greatly expand the range of teaching, learning, and communication modalities available to teachers and students, but at bottom their only value is in helping us to do other things well—engage students deeply in a topic, help them take more responsibility for their learning, help them learn to communicate clearly about their work and their ideas.

Yet, for a variety of reasons, educational technologies tend to draw our attention until they seem to be the most important thing in the picture. Fixated on new technologies, excited by their capabilities, or preoccupied with their new demands, we forget the far more important relationships and interactions that the technologies are in schools and in classrooms to support.

The purpose of this chapter is to put back into focus the human side of the educational equation, the goals and aims that we have as teachers for our students. What kinds of knowledge, what forms of interaction, what habits of mind and of work do we want to foster in students? And how might new media, taken broadly, serve or not serve these most basic and most important of goals?

Our intention in this chapter is to "come clean" about our biases as authors—the particular vision of schooling that underlies our discussions in this book of the uses of new technologies and new media and related media literacy issues. This vision is not ours alone, but is broadly shared by reform-minded educators nationwide; and it is not pure bias, but is based on a large amount of developmental and educational research into how children learn well in a variety of disciplines. First, however, we should explain why it is important to be clear about educational visions, goals, and biases when talking about the use of technologies in schools.

◆ Technologies Are Tools

Yes, technologies are tools, but for what ends? To use them well, we must be clear about the educational and human purposes we want them to serve. Computers and network technologies have been and are now being used for very different educational ends. Consider these two scenarios:

At James Madison High School in New York City, tenth-grade students, mostly African American and Latino, file into a networked computer lab and find seats at large new monitors and keyboards. Outside, in the hallways, in the stairwells, and in the foyers, the school resembles a minimum-security-prison facility, with metal detectors at the doors, a police substation located off the foyer, and security guards who move through the halls breaking up small groups of students who are avoiding classes by lounging on stairs and in rest rooms. James Madison is a large school in a middle-income neighborhood, but nearly all the students are poor and working-class. Drugs and violence are a recurrent problem. The computer lab, however, is a relative haven: it is quiet here, and as students enter their names into the computer, they find that the software program greets them warmly by name, remembers exactly where they were when they left off the day before with their work, and gently guides them through well-designed exercises in biology, algebra, and American history, praising successful answers and offering patient prompting and another chance—without a hint of judgment—when they miss an answer. The teacher, who monitors the students' individual workstations from a central machine of his own, moves around the room, helping students with technical problems, finding files, and printing. The students work well and mostly silently until the bell rings fifty minutes after they entered the room. Then they file out to return to their regular classrooms where, despite some dedicated teachers, the crowded, noisy, and sometimes intimidating teaching conditions will ensure that they remain relatively anonymous, and will have little contact with challenging material. In the chaotic context of James Madison, technology is the vehicle of a more individualized, effective—and possibly humane—instruction than students might otherwise get.

At the Richmond Academy, a private school across town from James Madison, ninth-graders file into their social studies classroom and, before class begins, log on to one of six workstations at tables against the walls. They argue noisily about what they are finding as they unearth an archaeological site in ancient Greece. The students have been working on the computer-based archaeology simulation for about three weeks, and teams of students are each responsible for excavating one of four separate quadrants of the site. It is a welcome break for the ninth-graders, who in their other classes spend much of their time taking lecture notes and learning to parse sophisticated texts as part of their college-prep curriculum. Here they are "digging up" pottery shards, fragments of weapons, pieces of masonry, and bits of ancient texts, and trying to identify and interpret each artifact in order to fit it into their emerging picture of the site as a whole. In their research the students visit local museums, consult reference works on Greek history, art, and architecture, and ask other teachers in the school to help translate texts. Cleverly, the students' teachers have filled the site with ambiguous evidence, so that some teams find a preponderance of data suggesting the site was a temple, while others find artifacts mostly suggesting it was a battlefield. In weekly meetings the teams present their latest findings to the rest of the class, and a hot debate ensues as the amateur archaeologists struggle to reconcile the fragmentary and ambiguous data. On this day the classroom is active and noisy, yet controlled, as students take turns at the computer, graph their findings on large wall-charts, call across the room to ask if anyone has a spearhead to compare with one just found, and argue about whose final interpretation of the site will best explain the bulk of the evidence.

In both of these settings the computers are state-of-the-art; in both they are being used for valid educational ends; and in both they are contributing positively to the educational needs of the students. While the school contexts are in sharp contrast—a large urban public high school serving low-income students, and a well-endowed private prep school serving elite students—by itself this contrast only underscores that technologies, as flexible tools, can meet very different needs, and can meet them well. At James Madison the computer-based curriculum manages to individualize, streamline, and even humanize learning in an otherwise chaotic, depersonalized school setting. At Richmond Academy, the computer-based simulation challenges students to develop skills beyond those of processing texts, and to learn to "read" and reason from images, architecture, and art about cultures distant in time and place. All in all, the computer as a "tool" appears to be used appropriately, given the different goals that define success for students in these two settings.

Indeed, educators in both schools cite their computer-based classes as models of "information-age schooling," schooling "for the twenty-first century." What do these slogans mean? Most important is the implicit idea that students are gaining skills they will need to be successful in a technology-infused workplace. This is perhaps the most frequently heard rationale for why schools must integrate new technologies. On their face, both claims appear to be true: students at James Madison and Richmond are immersed in computer learning environments every day and are becoming familiar with keyboarding and computer "navigation" skills, simulations, computer modeling, multimedia presentations, and more. This kind of technological literacy, in addition to the subject matter knowledge they gain, should stand them in good stead in an economy where technologies are a common feature of the workplace.

◆ Instructional Delivery vs. Inquiry

It can be argued, then, that both schools described above are preparing their students for work in the high-tech job market of the twenty-first century. By looking more closely, however, we can see that the scenarios presented above represent two very distinct visions for technology use in schools, two different visions of teaching and learning, and, very possibly, two different sets of life outcomes for students.

The first vision, represented by the James Madison computer lab, can be called the instructional delivery model. In it:

- ◆ learning is understood narrowly, as the mastery of discrete facts and bodies of information;
- ◆ technology functions as a delivery mechanism—a clean and efficient means of achieving content mastery;
- ◆ software contains the material to be learned and guides the learning process;
- ◆ students interact primarily with software and not with other students or adults;
- ◆ teachers are relegated to a relatively small role as monitors of learning;
- ◆ subject matter and performance criteria are predetermined and remain unquestioned; and
- ◆ use of the technology can be incorporated within the existing structure and with little or no impact on the larger organization of teaching and learning in the school.

The computer lab at James Madison, with its integrated learning system, organizes work along the lines of a successful factory, one that seeks to optimize the efficiency with which individual students progress in the mastery of discrete skills and bodies of information. The fact that at James Madison and schools like it, the factory model of schooling is a more personal and individualized form of instruction than students otherwise get should not obscure the traditional and conservative nature of this form of instruction. This is the model of instruction that has held sway in American schools for most of the twentieth century, based on rote learning of preestablished material. In it there is little room for students' own questions, concerns, or prior ways of understanding material; thinking is oriented to finding the right answer among a preselected set of options; and students have few opportunities to learn from others, whose ideas and learning strategies may be different from theirs.

But aren't students at least being prepared for the high-tech workplace? True, students at Madison are gaining exposure to varieties of computer applications; but they do so as relatively passive absorbers of information, not as active thinkers and inquirers. In the high-tech workplace they will have been prepared to perform relatively routine jobs like data entry and monitoring computer-controlled procedures. They will not have gained the ability to learn continuously, think complexly about problems, and devise creative solutions within real-world constraints—skills that workplaces often prize and reward. Added to this, recent analyses of the high-tech economy suggest that in it, more jobs are being created for business managers and professionals who are trained to evaluate options and make decisions in complex problem-settings than are being created for high-technology workers.[1] The ability to use one's mind flexibly and well remains a far better guarantee of workplace success than facility with the latest technology.

By contrast, the second vision of teaching and learning, reflected in the Richmond students' simulated archaeological dig, can be called the inquiry model. In it:

◆ learning is understood broadly, as the ability to use one's mind well in framing and solving open-ended problems in original ways, and in coordinating complex activities with others;

◆ technology serves as a catalyst and support for an extended classroom inquiry that is open-ended and "messy," involving guessing, debate, and multiple materials;

◆ technology serves limited roles and is integrated with other tools and media—students learn using many different resources, including books, libraries, museums, videos, and adult experts, in the school and beyond;

◆ students work collaboratively (and competitively) in teams, helping each other to learn and sharing data in ways that model how real scientists collaborate;

◆ teachers play crucial roles in selecting goals and materials, and as guides and intellectual coaches to students;

◆ broad subject matter decisions are made by teachers and more local ones by students, and teachers give students a role in determining performance criteria;

◆ the use of technology challenges the dominant mode of text-driven instruction in the school, making it more inquiry-based, collaborative, and varied in the use of resources.

Put simply, the contrast between these two visions of education and technology use can be summarized by saying that the first one seeks an efficient mechanism for the delivery of instruction, while the second seeks a rich environment in which students can learn to use their minds well.

◆ A Disturbing Divide

Not surprisingly, teaching children to use their minds well has most often been a value in public and private schools serving relatively elite students, where educators are given some flexibility in defining what and how students learn and resources exist to support enriched learning activities. In contrast, efficiency in delivering pre-set curriculum has been a value in public school systems serving middle-class, working-class, and poor communities, where public pressure for accountability over tight tax dollars lessens the autonomy and resources with which educators can work. As a result, the use of computers as flexible classroom tools to support collaborative inquiry learning is relatively uncommon, occurring most often in those relatively few and relatively affluent schools that stress thinking, that give teachers adequate resources to work with, and that support ongoing professional development for teachers. Far more common in large, bureaucratically driven public schools is the use of technology as a delivery mechanism. Hence the proliferation of computer labs, of integrated learning systems, of classroom computers used only to access CD-ROM encyclopedias, drill and practice games, "infotainment," word processing, and, now, "research on the Internet."

These may or may not be valid purposes for computers in schools. But one thing seems clear: given the gap in educational aims and means so common among American schools—the bulk of which teach for rote mastery of information amid conditions of relative scarcity, while a few teach students to use their minds well amid relative plenty—technology uses like these will do little to challenge a vast and growing gap in intellectual capital between our nation's schoolchildren. How can we make rigorous-inquiry learning more widespread in American schools, and how can technologies help level the playing field instead of widen the gap between rich and poor? This inherent problem in our democracy can be addressed only by linking three things—the movement for school reform, new insights about teaching and learning, and judicious and appropriate uses of technologies.

◈ The Challenge: Linking School Reform, Inquiry Teaching, and New Technologies

In the past ten to fifteen years a national school reform movement has sought to address the failings of large, bureaucratically driven schools by pushing for smaller, more intimate schools and reduced class sizes, greater responsibility for teachers in decisions over curriculum and budget, more flexibility in evaluation and assessment, and greater responsiveness and connection to parents and local communities. The Coalition for Essential Schools, James Comer's School-Family Partnerships, the Annenberg rural and urban school initiatives, large-scale reform efforts in Chicago, Philadelphia, the San Francisco Bay Area and New York, and the growing number of charter schools across the country are just a few examples of this movement. The animating idea behind these initiatives is that where students are well known as individuals, where teachers work together from a shared educational vision, where students are trusted to take responsibility for their learning and are held to high standards of accountability, where parents are deeply involved in the school community, and where decisions about assessment are collectively and publicly made, students of all backgrounds can and will learn at high levels of achievement.

At the same time, an emerging body of developmental and cognitive research has led to a growing consensus about the ways children learn well, and this consensus has begun to change educators' views of how teaching and learning should be organized at the classroom level. Educators are now placing greater emphasis on students as active builders and testers of knowledge in and across the disciplines. Sometimes dubbed the "cognitive revolution" or "constructivism," this new consensus in fact recapitulates ideas developed by John Dewey and other early educational progressives about students as "active learners." The central insight, simply put, is that learners build powerful maps of the world only by starting from and adding to or revising their existing maps, or schemas. Students, therefore, need opportunities to formulate, test, and revise their concepts about the world and its phenomena, whether human, mathematical, or scientific. The work that teachers do to support students' active testing, revising, and extending of concepts is sometimes called, in educational jargon, "scaffolding." This term reflects the fact that teachers let students—like construction workers on a scaffold—perform the essential task of building knowledge but provide a rich and carefully crafted learning environment to support them in their work. The "scaffold" may include direct teaching of certain key information, ideas, or skills, and the provision of key materials and resources, but it must leave room for students to tinker, speculate, create, and revise. And the scaffolding of ideas takes place best in a human and social context of discussion, debate, and comparison of one's own "maps" with those of others.

Armed with this view of teaching and learning, professional educators' groups such as the National Association for Teachers of Mathematics, the National Science Teachers Association, and the National Center for History in the Schools are busy revising curriculum and drafting national standards that are becoming models for state and local standards around the country. While they push for deeper, more active, and rigorous teaching in the disciplines, the new standards are philosophically in sync with the aims of the school reform community. In particular, they suggest the need for schools to provide teachers with greater autonomy and support than they have had to date, including flexibility in shaping curriculum and assessment, less instructional time and more planning time, opportunities for block-scheduling and team-teaching, and ongoing professional development opportunities.

Finally, there is a growing recognition that technologies must be enlisted in support of changed instructional practices and invigorated school communities. The recognition is evident in many places. Conference panels and presentations on technology and school reform are now more common than ever.[2] School reform people, having spent ten years (appropriately) focused on community-building and governance issues, are now focusing on classroom practices and, in particular, ways technologies can support school cultures of inquiry and reflection. And on their side, educational technologists have understood that in order for media to have meaningful and lasting impact in schools they must be adopted in tandem with changes in school culture and organization, not simply grafted onto existing practices. Reflecting this shift in perspective, in 1995 the magazine *Electronic Learning,* long an advocate of school technology, added to its name the subtitle "the magazine of technology and school reform."

Increasingly, educators and technologists—including the authors of this book—are arguing that technologies need to be integrated into schools in service of inquiry-based pedagogies and need to be supported by a changed organization of schooling. As a result, academics and practitioners have sought to align the goals of school reform with the functions and capabilities of new technologies. In this chapter we discussed three key ways technologies can support work in these changed schools: as research tools, as production tools, and as conversational tools. Now we highlight features of emerging schools that link inquiry teaching, new technologies, and school reform.

◆ Democratic, Information-Age Schools

These concepts come together in a vision of democratic, information-age schools—schools that will not only prepare students to

be successful in the workplace, but also prepare them to participate actively as citizens in their communities. Prototypes of such
schools exist—and not just in wealthy communities, but in lower-
income urban and rural communities as well. As schools such as
the celebrated Central Park East schools in New York City's East
Harlem attest, schools need not be technology rich to be "information-age." Rather, the phrase "information-age" signals that
the schools focus on developing students' critical habits of mind
with regard to ideas and evidence—the ability to use their minds
well. Technologies, however, while not the key ingredients in
these schools, do have important roles to play in them.

◆ Six Attributes of a Democratic, Information-Age School

Researchers have suggested at least six features that distinguish
democratic, information-age schools. Here is how Vicki Hancock,
a curriculum supervisor who has traveled extensively documenting these features of new schools, describes them:

- *Interactivity.* In schools demonstrating interactivity, students communicate with other students through formal
  presentations, cooperative learning activities, and informal dialogue. Students and teachers talk to one another
  about their learning tasks in large groups, small groups,
  and one-to-one. Students have constant access to and
  know how to use print and electronic information resources to inform their learning activities. They recognize the value of the information in their own
  communities and interact with various community
  members, including businesspeople, social service staff,
  arts professionals, athletes, older adults, and volunteer
  workers.
- *Self-initiated learning.* When students initiate their own
  learning, they participate in productive questioning,
  probing for information they can use rather than waiting for the next question on a test or from a teacher.
  Information resources are central, not peripheral, in
  day-to-day learning activities. Students gather their

own data to learn about topics, using a variety of sources and practicing effective research techniques. They are able to examine the large quantity of information they have gathered, synthesize it, and reduce it to usable quantities for their purposes. They can analyze and interpret information in the context of the problems or questions they have identified, and they can evaluate not only the quality of the information they've gathered, but also the processes they've used to gather it.

◆ *A changing role for teachers.* To develop self-initiated learners in the information-age school, the teacher's role must evolve away from dispenser of prefabricated facts to coach and guide. In this continuously changing role, teachers leave fact-finding to the computer, spending their time doing what they were meant to do as content experts: arousing curiosity, asking the right questions at the right time, and stimulating debate and serious discussion around engaging topics. In fact, every adult in the school community communicates the power of knowledge by modeling a love of learning. Pre-service and in-service programs require the use of information resources and technologies as an integrated part of teachers' certification and recertification. Teachers create a community among themselves in which they are willing to plan together, share successes, resolve challenges, and model strategies for one another.

◆ *Media and technology specialists as central participants.* Media and technology specialists are critical in the information-age school, and their role is twofold. Working with students, they are project facilitators. They can ask the initial questions that help students develop a focus for inquiry. They are thoroughly familiar with the school's and district's information resources and can direct students to multidisciplinary materials suitable for their investigations. With their technology skills they can assist students in their efforts to develop technology-enhanced products and presentations. Working with teachers, they are instructional designers—partners in curriculum development and unit planning. Their expertise with information resources can inform teachers' exploration of curriculum topics and assist them in locating the materials they need. And, because ongoing professional development is an integral part of the work in an information-age school, media and technology specialists contribute their expertise to the design and delivery of technology-enhanced in-service programs.

◆ *Continuous evaluation.* Everyone in the information-age school recognizes the need for continuous evaluation is not limited to scheduled standardized assessments. They engage in a high level of introspection, asking questions about the appropriateness of information resources, the efficiency of information searches, and the quality of information selection and evaluation. They also examine the quality of the products and presentations they use to share the results of their inquiries, as well as the communication process itself.

◆ *A changed environment.* An information-age school has a different look and feel from a traditional school. Classroom methods link information retrieval, analysis, and application with strategies such as cooperative learning, guided inquiry, and thematic teaching. Information technologies are easily accessible, not locked away in media closets or labs. Student projects and products proliferate—not just as display items but as resources for other students and information for future investigations. Classrooms and hallways are frequently the scene of discussions and debates about substantive issues—topics important to both the curriculum and to the students investigating them. Most important, the most probing questions come from the learners, who are curious about a variety of issues and intent on communicating what they discover: How do you know that? What evidence do you have for that? Who says? How can we find out?[3]

A Seventh Attribute: Critical Media Literacy

In addition to the six attributes of the information-age school de-scribed by Vicki Hancock, we must add a seventh: habits of criti-cal reflection on the impacts of media themselves—including educational technologies—on our lives and our learning. Media literacy is an important part of being a productive and effective citizen in a media-saturated world, and it is an especially impor-tant adjunct to the use of new technologies in the information-rich classroom.

In information-age schools, students and teachers alike reflect critically on mass media messages and experiences with new tech-nologies, asking whose point of view is being expressed, what in-terests or motivations are represented, how the form of the message or product affects our reception of it, and whether it can be judged an accurate, balanced, or distorted presentation. Such media literacy is crucial in our contemporary world, where prob-lems, ideas, and arguments find complex representation in an ever-wider variety of media forms and channels, and has an espe-cially important place in an information-rich school.

Helping students move from relatively passive absorption of information to habits in which they are able to frame arguments, consider evidence, and apply judgment creatively is key if we are to develop powerful and flexible thinkers capable of communicat-ing about and solving difficult problems.

Changes Needed in the Organization of Schooling

In closing, it is important to underscore again the changes in school organization that will be necessary in order for the activi-ties and values of information-age schooling discussed in this chapter to take root and thrive in schools, supported by new tech-nologies. To see why, briefly consider the way learning is orga-nized at the Educational Video Center, described in Chapter 1. At EVC, classes are typically:

- driven by students' social and cultural interests and ques-tions across disciplines;
- based on information drawn from a range of print, visual,

Media Literacy—Key Habits of Mind

Media or information literacy embraces the following considerations, whether one is composing one's own media text or responding to another.

What	What's the main idea? What picture of the world is being presented? What argument is being made?
Who	Whose point of view is it? What does the author want the viewer/reader/user to think or do?
Evidence	What facts or information are offered in support of the argument or idea? How relevant and reliable is the information?
Style	What's the form of the presentation? What genre is it? How is the message conveyed via words, images, sounds?
Audience	Who are the intended viewers/readers/users? How might they or other audiences respond?
Representation	What people and what subjects are represented, and how? Are the portrayals of people or other subjects accurate, exaggerated, biased?
What else?	What questions do I have now? What other points of view might be included? What additional information do I need, and where can I get it?

and community sources and not from a standard curriculum or mandated textbook;

◆ video- and computer-technology intensive;

◆ two or more hours long to allow for in-depth work, travel for shoots, etc.;

◆ taught through a range of visual, oral, and print-based languages;

◆ designed for fewer than fifteen students per teacher;

◆ assessed by performance standards and portfolios.

Many if not most of these practices run counter to what administrators, teachers, and parents consider to be practical or good education—what has been called "real school."[4] For example, video work that requires teams of students to leave the building for hours at a time may not fit with a school schedule built around students moving through discrete classes at fifty-minute intervals. A topic like "our city's unequal schools" that is of interest to students may be viewed as inappropriate because it is not part of any established curriculum or standardized test. Likewise, teachers may not see the value of analyzing photographs or television commercials as part of developing visual literacy skills, because they have to prepare students for exams in literature. Video may not be seen as a valid medium of student work because it cannot be assessed using standard evaluation practices. Teachers who are unfamiliar with the video medium but want to learn about it may be unable to because their school does not provide sufficient time for faculty development, nor the support of a media specialist who knows how to help teachers integrate media into instruction.

Some of the key areas that schools will need to change in order to support more democratic, information-age instruction, include:

◆ *Greater autonomy and trust for teachers and students.* Within a general framework of agreed-upon curriculum standards, teachers need to be given responsibility for key decisions about exactly what curriculum is taught and via what strategies and approaches. Students, too, must be trusted to take greater responsibility for their own learning, and left to make key choices about topics, resources, and methods of study. In both cases, teachers and students should be held accountable to high standards and must be able to justify their choices with reference to agreed-upon performance criteria.

◆ *Smaller schools and class sizes.* Schools must function as communities if adults and students are to have any hope of reaching consensus about educational goals and standards. So schools need to be small enough so that every student is well known, all the adults can meet productively in face-to-face meetings, and each adult has primary responsibility for no more than forty students. And because inquiry-based and collaborative learning requires close monitoring and coaching of students, class sizes need to be small.

- *Flexible- and block-scheduling.* Students' curiosity and in-depth project work rarely obey the fifty-minute hour and the neat division of subject matter into math, English, social studies, and science. For teachers to foster deep learning through meaningful student projects, they need the flexibility to experiment with interdisciplinary courses, block-scheduling, and team-teaching.

- *Alternative assessments.* Student projects that result in plays, performances, models, novels, videos, science experiments, Web sites, and other outcomes can rarely be evaluated using standardized tests. Further, as long as teachers are held accountable via standardized test scores, innovative practices of any kind will gain little foothold. As a result, schools need to experiment with alternatives to traditional assessment that invite teachers, administrators, and community members to define shared criteria for good performance. These include portfolio and performance assessments that display students' progress over time through concrete evidence, and "roundtable" assessments and reviews where multiple stake-holders, including parents, are at the table and students are given opportunities to explain and defend their work.

- *Media and technology support.* Classroom teachers cannot be expected to keep up with the latest software upgrades, understand the newest vogue in on-line interactions and its implications for classrooms, or guide students in HTML authoring. On-demand, school-based technology support is therefore crucial. But the most common organization of technology support in schools—the "media specialist" or "computer coordinator" who presides over the computer lab and has very little to do with teachers or curriculum—is a key barrier to successful technology integration. Schools need, instead, "media generalists"—staff members who are technically skilled but who are equally knowledgeable about curriculum and interpersonally skilled at working with teachers where the rubber meets the road—around students' use of technologies for subject-matter learning.

- *Ongoing faculty development.* Above all, schools need to provide teachers with ongoing professional development opportunities. Teachers need to be supported in taking risks and adopting new instructional strategies. Existing models of staff development that stress one-time workshops with occasional group brushups are wholly inadequate to the demands of changing complex instructional practices, including those involving new media tools. Teachers need to be given time and support to approach a new practice as learners, gradually experiment with aspects of the new practice in the classroom, and continuously reflect on the meaning and value of the innovation with other teachers. On-line technologies themselves have roles to play in this process, linking teachers in safe and supportive learning communities in which they can reflect with one another on their learning as they adopt new instructional strategies and resources.

By moving forward with these changes in school organization, supporting teachers as they adopt teaching practices oriented toward helping students use their minds flexibly and well, and integrating media tools in a thoughtful and critical fashion, educators and policymakers will have taken a big step toward making the democratic, information-age schooling a reality for all children.

NOTES

1. L. Uchitelle. "Study questions the usual view of downsizing." *The New York Times*. February 10, 1998. p. D1.

2. Cf. Wingspread Conference on Media, Arts, and School Reform. Racine, Wisconsin, October 1996. Also, the Coalition of Essential Schools Fall Forum in San Francisco, November 1997.

3. V. Hancock. "Creating the Information Age School." *Educational Leadership*. Association for Supervision and Curriculum Development. November 1997.

4. D. Tyack and L. Cuban. *Tinkering Toward Utopia: A Century of School Reform.* (Baltimore, Md.: Johns Hopkins University Press, 1996).

· 3 ·

New Media in the History and Social Studies Classroom

◆ New Technologies and History: Finding the Link

Why use new technologies in the history and social studies classroom? What important roles can they play in helping students gain a deep, flexible, well-reasoned, and personally meaningful understanding of history and the social world? To answer these questions comprehensively would require a book dedicated solely to that task, because there are so many different goals in history and social studies teaching to consider, and so many different kinds of media that can be used to address them. For our purposes, a sensible alternative is to review some of the *changes* currently under way in history teaching and to highlight several features of new media that can support these changes in significant ways.

From Neat History to Messy History

History teaching is changing. Broadly stated, the change can be described as a shift from neat history to messy history. Neat history is characterized by a coherent, agreed-upon, linear narrative, and by delivery systems such as textbooks and lecture-and-slide presentations. In fact, textbooks are the quintessentially "neat" form of history.

History textbooks, when you think about it, do a lot of work. They survey the historical research, carefully select and arrange the agreed-upon stories within a comprehensible framework, and present them all in age-appropriate language and an eye-appealing format. The trouble is that all of this work and neatness leaves the student—the learner—with relatively little to do except to read carefully and try to absorb as much of the narrative and as many of the explanatory ideas as possible. Students learning textbook history are the passive consumers of history as a neat end-product, a set of agreed-upon and well-presented stories. All too often what they take away, in addition to whatever names, events, and ideas they remember, is a firm belief that history is boring—a closed book.

In contrast, the more messy history being undertaken in many classrooms looks a lot like the messy work done by professional historians: students pose speculative questions, browse in old archives, mull over old photographs, collect oral histories, propose speculative answers, argue and debate interpretations with others, role-play, write and publish monographs, and even write historical fiction. In all of these activities we can recognize qualities that are central to the curricular reforms we have discussed earlier—qualities of student-centeredness, active learning, and a focus on inquiry. Yet, rather than simply accepting that these are good or inevitable practices in the history classroom, it is worth asking why this shift toward more messy history is occurring, and why it is important.

Why the Shift to Messy History?

Three intersecting developments underlie and support the shift toward more messy history: 1) a perceived crisis in students' knowledge of history; 2) a new view of American history, and 3) changes in the media with which we store, retrieve, and disseminate our cultural memory.

The Failure of "Neat" History

The first development is the discovery that neat history taught from textbooks simply hasn't worked well. Since the mid-1980s, educators and policymakers have been pointing to American students' startling lack of basic historical knowledge, and arguing for a series of reforms.[1] Suggestions have been to return history to a more central place in the curriculum, to reemphasize narrative and the power of stories (as against what are viewed as the vague and present-minded concepts of social studies), to engage students with the histories of more diverse cultures and peoples, and to emphasize the development of historical thinking skills through the use of primary sources.[2]

Common to all these calls to improve history education is a belief that a democratic society needs citizens who not only know some history but can use and apply it carefully in thinking through contemporary problems in society and in their own lives. There is consensus that classrooms, therefore, need to cultivate students' moral imaginations in relation to past events and peoples as well as their content knowledge of historical events. In short, history classrooms need to be enlivened with rich forms of narrative, critical work with sources, and lots of argument and debate.

History from Multiple Perspectives

The second development underlying the shift to more messy history is a new view of American history arising from recent scholarship. In the past thirty years historians have created whole new subdisciplines of historical scholarship—labor history, immigrant history, women's history, African American history—and in doing so have radically altered our understanding of the American past. No longer a document of strictly political, economic, and military figures, ideas, and events, U.S. history now includes *social* history, the complex record of how ordinary Americans from many backgrounds both experienced and shaped the American experiment. The result is a richer, more complex, and more multivocal view of the past. Significantly, this is a history that has the potential to speak much more clearly to the diverse students in American classrooms today.

For teachers, however, this new view of history poses significant challenges. For one thing, it means an increase in the voices and perspectives that need to be included in the American story.

Teachers who already struggle to "cover" an enormous range of material must now contend with the need to expose students to multiple perspectives on the past. Moreover, the proliferation of voices and perspectives makes it difficult to give students a single coherent version of the American story. (This is not something that teachers struggle with alone. One feature of the cultural moment is that a coherent narrative eludes museum curators, documentary makers, writers, and others whose job it is to speak to a broad public about the American past.) Textbooks reflect this difficulty, with their sidebars, boxes, and special sections that focus on the contributions of different groups and yet sit uneasily next to the main text. Similar problems can be seen in embattled museum exhibitions such as the Smithsonian Institution's *Enola Gay* exhibit of the early 1990s.

The problem is often posed as a need to choose which of two narratives ought to be the dominant or "the right one." Yet despite popular demand for single, simple story lines, this is not the way historians view history. They see historical change as the sum of overlapping and sometimes contradictory influences, and see its meanings refracted through many different eyes. It is this more complex and many-sided history that teachers must aim to help students grasp. In this chapter we try to identify some ways that new media can help.

History in Multiple Media

The third development behind the more messy history is based on changes in the way we store, retrieve, and share the historical materials that constitute our cultural memory. Two large trends can be distinguished: the gradual move to more visual materials, and the growth of digital storage and retrieval of both print and nonprint materials.

Since the invention at the end of the nineteenth century of technologies for reproducing imagery on a mass scale, the image has moved to an ever more central place in our culture. Now, at the close of the twentieth century, it is fair to say that the image rivals the word as the primary mode of public address, the medium in which collective life is enacted and expressed. This has meant that more and more historical materials are taking the form of nontextual materials, including photographs, films, videos, advertisements, and audio of speeches, radio programs, etc. Historians must now be adept at working with all of these materials, and more. And so must students if we want them to grasp history with any of the nuance and complexity we have described above. There is every reason to think that students will find interpreting visual materials a compelling part of their historical investigations, yet they are seldom given a chance to develop such skills. In part, this has been the result of the scarcity of such materials in classrooms.

In the Web-connected history classroom at least, this scarcity of rich historical materials may soon give way to abundance, fulfilling one of the promises of the digital revolution. This is because many of the nation's large university and government libraries and archives, which, after all, are custodians of much of the nation's past, have been putting large collections of historical and cultural materials on-line; relatively free of added costs. Thus, in addition to the commercially published multimedia encyclopedias available on CD-ROM, teachers and students with Web access can tap into more and more on-line historical archives.

It is difficult to overstate the dramatic increase in public access this gradual digitization of the nation's heritage represents. Many of these raw historical materials—primary sources that include pamphlets, diaries, photographs, oral histories, films, speeches, playscripts, maps, etc.—have not been available before now to any but the small handful of researchers and scholars who could afford to travel to the library or archive and spend hours or days searching through handwritten indexing systems and poring over the actual documents. Beyond making archival materials available, digital media such as the World Wide Web also make available the range of views and opinions that a divided and contentious public holds about historical matters.

In sum, it is important to see the more active, messy kind of history-learning now beginning to take hold in classrooms as something more than an attempt to find the most effective way of teaching history. In fact, we can see messy history as an attempt to acknowledge and address a series of broader changes in our understanding of how children learn, in historical scholarship, in the media with which we store the records of our past, and in our polyglot society as a whole. History is everywhere a more complex and messy affair. There are more voices and perspectives in the mix, more complex models of how groups of people have interacted and struggled to produce historical change, and more varied records of our cultural conversations.

From this perspective, the pedagogic strategies that we have described in the earlier chapters appear as key tools with which to make social studies and history learning more intellectually rigorous, and more socially and personally relevant for today's diverse students. Active and collaborative learning activities (role-playing, simulations, etc.) combined with student-centered inquiry (students formulating questions, gathering data, producing reports) combined with authentic materials (primary sources, oral histories) offer opportunities for students to become deeply engaged in the historical enterprise as an ongoing democratic effort to create a better and more just life for themselves and for others around them.

New Technologies in the History Classroom: Where Do They Fit?

Now that we have sketched the new "messy" history classroom and some of the developments behind it, it is possible to ask how and where new technologies fit into the mix. We can ask the question in these ways:

- How can new media tools help engage students intellectually and affectively in both historical narrative and in active historical investigation?
- How can they provide access to multiple kinds of evidence and multiple perspectives on historical processes?
- How can they support students' efforts to develop the kinds of complex understandings of history that are now necessary?

Posing the question of where technologies fit in these terms immediately allows us to make two observations.

First, we can see that some forms of historical materials, though utilizing new media, do not serve these aims well at all. CD-ROMs or Web sites that present broad sweeps of history in multimedia format (meaning there are occasional photos, film clips, or sound clips included) often resemble the decontextualized encyclopedia entries that students have always used in preparing "reports." Historical films that dramatize past events often simplify the events greatly, and offer teachers and students little means of judging the adequacy of the historical interpretation they present.

Second, we can see that no materials, by themselves, could accomplish these aims for students. To engage students' emotions, to help them understand multiple perspectives, to help them develop critical skills with sources—all of these require adults who frame the use of resources in careful and creative ways. Teachers can present an interesting historical film such as Ken Burns's Civil War series, for example, as a definitive account of the war, or they can ask students as they watch to look for evidence of the way average soldiers, in contrast to generals, or men in contrast to women, or whites in contrast to blacks, experienced the war. In the first instance students watch relatively passively, and attend only to those elements to which they are individually attuned. After viewing a film in this way, most students will probably have trouble discussing or forming an opinion about the filmmaker's overall perspective on the topic, in this case the war. In the second instance students might be asked to take notes while they watch, jotting down key phrases under columns headed Officers/Soldiers, Men/Women, or Whites/Blacks. Discussing the film afterward, they would be able to refer to their notes as they try together to characterize some of the differences in perspective, a difficult but important task. This kind of active viewing would also help them assess how the filmmaker views the war—as the crucible through which the American *pluribus* was made *unum*.

As always, resources in no way determine the quality of an educational experience; they simply provide teachers and students with greater or lesser opportunities for building rich learning experiences. Our task, then, is to identify which features or genres of new media might enrich history-learning in the ways specified above.

For purposes of this discussion we can note four major kinds of technology tools that hold particular promise for enabling messy history in the ways above:

1) On-line archives of historical materials
2) On-line communication forums

3) Composition and publishing tools
4) Historical simulations

Each of these media genres has unique characteristics, and can offer distinctive benefits in the history classroom.

On-line historical archives offer access to primary sources in many novel formats and allow novices to undertake the advanced kinds of inquiry that scholars normally do, while bringing their own questions and concerns to bear. Communications forums on the Web enable students to participate in the ongoing construction of historical meaning with a wide assortment of other people. Composition and publishing tools such as computers and camcorders enable students to visualize historical complexity and change, and develop and express their understanding of the ways that personal and local history connect to history on a larger scale. And historical simulations place students "back in time," not simply to drink up the atmosphere of a different period, but to role-play and problem-solve, and in doing so develop historical knowledge and skills. While each of the genres has its unique aspects, however, together they share a single important quality: their capacity to help students develop a more committed, personal stake in historical investigation and storytelling.

In the following section, we briefly discuss each of the media genres above, in order to clarify their relation to a more messy, dynamic, and rigorous history classroom.

Media Genres in the History Classroom

On-line Historical Archives

What are on-line archives? How are they different from other media? And what makes them particularly useful in the history classroom? On-line archives as we mean them here are large collections of nonproprietary historical and cultural material that can be accessed via the Web. Generally speaking, such archives are made available by government libraries and museums, and research universities—institutions whose mission includes the collection and preservation of historical and scholarly materials. Examples of historical and cultural archives that are currently on-line include the following:

The American Memory Collections
Primary source collections from the Library of Congress.
http://memory.loc.gov

The National Archives' Digital Classroom
Digitized primary sources and teaching resources for K–12 ed-
    ucators.
http://www.nara.gov/education/classrm.html

The Valley of the Shadow Archive
Archives of two towns during the Civil War, from the Univer-
    sity of Virginia.
http://jefferson.village.virginia.edu/vshadow2/

The New Deal Network
Primary documents and teaching resources on the Depression
    and FDR.
http://newdeal.feri.org

Letters Home from a Civil War Soldier
http://www.ucsc.edu/civil-war-letters/home.html

THOMAS
Database of congressional proceedings
http://thomas.loc.gov

On-line archives are different from published teaching materials in several ways, all connected to the fact that they were created
to preserve important historical materials for scholars, and not
necessarily students, to study. For that reason, they are vast and
imperfectly organized; they are accessed via sophisticated search
tools; and they consist of raw, mostly uncontextualized primary
materials. While these qualities create challenges for classroom
use, they also confer great advantages in comparison to other
classroom materials for promoting the deep understanding that
comes with messy history.

The vastness and imperfect organization of these archives require students and teachers to undertake a process of searching
and selection to locate documents that are relevant to an inquiry.
Typically an initial student search can yield hundreds of "hits,"
only a few of which will be useful and interesting for the students'
purposes, while the bulk need to be discarded as irrelevant. Large

databases thus require—and can help develop in students—the ability to search, find, evaluate, and use information resources, what the library community has come to call "information literacy." In the history classroom the process of weeding out irrelevant documents is itself instructive, since it teaches that history involves selecting a small subset of material from the vast array of possible artifacts and crafting a story around these. Moreover, the size of many archives means that scholars cannot possibly have exhausted the historical data held in them. As we will see, students' questions may be as relevant as those of professional historians in querying a large body of primary historical material.

To find the materials they need in a large archive, students and teachers generally make use of electronic search tools and finding aids. While these tools sometimes map imperfectly onto a collection's cataloguing structure, they are powerful and can be used by students to query collections in novel ways.

The WPA Life Histories on the Library of Congress's American Memory Web site, for example, contain thousands of oral history interviews with ordinary Americans taken during the Depression, and they can be searched via any key words that users think of. This means students can search on terms of interest to them—terms that might not occur to a historian. In an assignment to find differences between life in the United States in the 1930s and life today, one teacher reported that a student searching on the term "gas station" came up with forty-six interviews with people who used the term. Sifting through these documents, the student put together a paper arguing that in contrast to today, gas stations during the 1930s functioned as a combination newsstand and social club.[3]

Other students searching on the term "sex" (of obvious interest to teens) zeroed in on three revealing interviews: one with an Italian immigrant cobbler discussing his worries about his daughter dating in the New World; one with a young woman who described the need to use her sexuality to get and keep a job in a factory; and one with a southern aristocratic woman talking about behaviors that were required for "the fairer sex." The students used these documents in a presentation that described the ways in which people's concerns about sex and sexuality in the

1930s were both similar to and different from their concerns today.

These are just two examples of the ways students can use large on-line collections and the search tools that go with them to discover unique and meaningful patterns in history based on their own interests.

The biggest educational advantage conferred by on-line archives is in the nature of the materials themselves. Primary source materials are distinguished from secondary materials in two main ways—they are vivid and they are incomplete.

Primary sources are firsthand accounts; they have a vividness for students and adults because they are so close to the events and circumstances they describe. At best they are local and personal, such as a letter, diary entry, or family photograph, and can offer students a glimpse into another person's experience of a remote time and place. Primary source archives can thus be very motivating for students to utilize, because they bring history up close as "the real thing."

Primary sources are also fragmentary. They do not tell the whole story; in fact, they offer only a fragment of the information needed to understand a historical event or issue and provide very little if any historical context. Why is this valuable in the history classroom? Because primary documents themselves do so little "telling" of history, students must themselves do the work of constructing a historical interpretation. The intellectual labor is on their shoulders primarily.

Here's an example that illustrates the value of those qualities. A typical primary document might be a soldier's ground-level description of a single day of a single battle. He might describe what he ate, the way the troops prepared for battle, the impressions he had once the fighting began, and his feelings about the aftermath of the conflict. His letter might never refer to the commanding general, the side he was fighting for, the name of the place where the battle occurred, or any other "historical" information. It certainly would not place the battle in historical context—explaining what led up to it, summarizing the battle as a whole, and explaining why it was significant in the course of the war. What do students get from working with the primary document, then? The answer is a rich and detailed case to contrast with other historical cases, and a series of questions to take to other materials. Students can understand something about the level of material culture at the time of the battle, something about the methods and technologies of warfare, something about the way an ordinary soldier viewed battle and the death of his comrades (as glorious or repugnant or simply necessary), perhaps something about the way he related to commanding officers and to his loved ones at home.

Students would almost certainly have more questions after such an encounter than answers. In this, they are prepared to conduct further research using other sources. In doing so, students learn about history as an ongoing process of making meaning from a fragmentary yet evolving body of evidence.

Finally, the "raw" nature of primary materials offers further advantages in the messy-history classroom. Primary materials in large archives are not edited to remove material that might be inflammatory or offensive by today's educational standards. Stereotypes of race, ethnicity, and nationality, for example, abound in such materials, for they have loomed large in our nation's past. Likewise, the messy details of history are available for all comers to see—the fact that many of our nation's early leaders held slaves, for example, or the details of slavery, or the propaganda that our nation has used to prepare for war, or the treatment of minorities, such as Japanese Americans, in periods of national crisis. The different points of view that have divided many Americans on issues of their day are more readily available in primary-source archives than in other teaching materials. These all fit well into a history classroom in which debate, contention, emotional engagement, and the continuing search to clarify one's moral stance on important issues have moved to the fore.

Dealing with Archival Documents: Developing Students' Visual Literacy

Students using on-line archives for historical study have access not only to documents that are more "raw" than most educational materials but also to historical documents that are in different media formats—photographs, political cartoons, pamphlets, audio files, films, and other physical artifacts, in addition to printed texts. To take advantage of these different kinds of documents, teachers and students need to learn new ways of querying primary sources, and, in particular, visual materials. As the historical record available through new media becomes a more visual and multimedia record, it becomes important for students and teachers to learn to see through and with images, to develop what might be called "visual literacy skills." In the history classroom this means treating photographs and films not simply as illustrations of past events and customs but as visual *evidence* for historical change. This section will explore this theme further, with examples.

At the beginning of a unit of study, primary sources can be used to stimulate students' interest and engagement in the topic to be studied. Used in this way, visual documents can act as catalysts to student thinking, discussion, and writing. This kind of warm-up activity can help a teacher clarify the group's level of prior knowledge and the questions students have about a period or event, and use these as a place from which to build.

Selecting a Primary Document

It is important to select an appropriately engaging image for students to examine. The following questions may be helpful in selecting primary documents:

- Is the document richly suggestive of the historical time and place?
- Does the content connect with students' interests and concerns?
- Is the language and imagery age-appropriate, i.e., is it accessible to students?
- Does the document raise larger social and historical themes? Can it help students develop the important social, historical, or political concepts they need to understand?
- Does the document contain evidence of the author's point of view or motivation?
- Are a variety of viewpoints or voices expressed in the document? If not, can I find supplementary resources that will help provide a balanced set of perspectives?

Applying these criteria to the photograph that follows makes it possible to see why this might be a good document for middle-school students to use in brainstorming about city life at the turn of the century. First, its content connects with students' interests and concerns (children are featured; there is a dead horse). Second, it is accessible to students of middle-school age (the objects and activities featured are fairly familiar; there is no text that is out of reach), and it is richly suggestive of its time and place (visible elements include wooden carriages, cobblestone streets, and an old streetlamp). Third, its subject matter reflects important aspects of the larger historical context, including urban poverty, poor sanitation, and risks to child welfare. Fourth, the photograph points to the activity of the photographer himself (quite literally, in the gesture of the little boy who is pointing at the camera), and thus invites speculation about his role and motivation.

Structuring Students' Encounter with the Visual Document

After selecting an engaging document, the next step is to loosely structure students' encounter with the document. In brainstorming, the goal is to get students engaged in the topic so that they generate their own ideas and questions about it rather than to teach any specific concepts or content. The best approaches tend to be those that allow students leeway in interpreting the document. However, in order to avoid merely subjective responses, it is important to have students spend a moment or two concentrating on what the document itself says or shows. A worksheet or student guide can be helpful here.

For a rich artifact like this photograph, the worksheet "History as Investigation" on the following page may be used to guide students in their analysis. The worksheet shapes the student's encounter with a historical document into four general steps, which may be done in order but which are ideally viewed as recursive steps.

The first step, observation, asks students to attend closely to what they read or see in the document, simply listing what is before them "on the surface" of the document. The second step, knowledge, asks students to consider what they already know

Web image: The close of a career in New York (1900–1910). (*Detroit Publishing Co. Photos, 1880–1921.*) http://memory.loc.gov

about the period, event, or topic of the document. The third step, conclusion, asks students what tentative conclusion they might draw about the meaning of the document or the world in which it was created. The fourth step, further research, asks students what else they need to know to understand the document or its world, what questions have arisen for them in the encounter, and where they might go to find more information.

The following example illustrates how the worksheet was used in a seventh grade social studies class studying immigration.

History as Investigation

OBSERVATION	KNOWLEDGE	CONCLUSION	FURTHER RESEARCH
Describe exactly what you see in the photo.	Summarize what you already know about the situation	Say what you conclude from what you see.	What questions has the photo raised? What are some

- What people and objects are shown?
- How are they arranged?
- What is the physical setting?
- What other details can you see?

and time period shown, and the people and objects that appear.

- What's going on in the picture?
- Who are the people and what are they doing?
- What is the function of the objects?
- What can we conclude about the time period?

sources I can use to find answers?

New Media in Action—Using a Photograph to Raise Questions About Urban Life: A Visual Literacy Activity

To introduce a lesson on urban life at the turn of the century, the teacher asked his students to examine the photo above. Titled *The Close of a Career,* it shows a street scene on the Lower East Side of New York City between 1900 and 1910. Students used the History as Investigation worksheet as a scaffold to guide their examination.

First, the teacher asked students to carefully *observe* as many things as possible that they see in the photo. Here are the things they wrote down:

Observation
- A dead horse
- A cobblestone street with puddles
- Six children, about 4 to 8 years old, sitting in the gutter nearby
- Some are playing a game.
- One is pointing (a stick? gun?).
- Two more older boys, standing up, one holding a stick
- A deep gutter
- Wooden carriages on the street and cart on sidewalk
- A run-down wooden fence and building (a house?)
- A warehouse or store, not wood
- A streetlamp
- Men standing in the distance

Next, students were asked what they already *know* about the time period of the picture and the things shown in it. Drawing on both personal and school knowledge, they said things such as:

Knowledge
- Dead animals can carry disease.
- Before there were cars, people used horse-drawn carriages.
- Before there was electricity, there was gas lighting.
- Sometimes kids used to work in factories.
- Not all children went to school.

Next, the seventh-graders were asked what they could tentatively *conclude* about what was happening in the photograph or about the period when it was taken. The things they wrote down included:

Conclusion
- There were no cars at the time.
- The horse probably pulled a wagon or carriage.
- It could have died from old age, starvation, or being sick.
- The kids playing in the street are poor.
- They don't have anyplace else to go.
- Children shouldn't be playing so close to a dead animal.
- The adults in the picture should be protecting the kids.

Finally, the students were asked to write down what questions they had and what research they thought they needed to do. They wrote down the following:

Further Research
- Why was the horse just left there?
- Will anybody pick it up? Who?
- Why don't they have a better place to play?
- Do they go to school?
- What kind of houses do they live in?
- Why don't the kids' parents, or other adults, keep them away from dangerous things like the horse?
- Where are the parents? What do they do?

What does this exercise tell us about the value of on-line historical archives in the social studies and history classroom? Most obviously, it supports the idea that access to primary-source materials helps students build their own historical knowledge rather than simply repeating what has been told to them. Further, it indicates the value of widening the scope of the materials students work with in the history classroom to include the visual historical record. Students were readily engaged with a well-chosen photograph on both the affective and intellectual levels. Finally, it suggests that teachers and students must learn new ways of working with the nontraditional documents that on-line archives make available. Images that have long functioned as illustrations in curriculum can now be treated as evidence, for example. The photo-analysis guide shown helps underscore the distinction between *observations* and *conclusions or interpretations,* as a way of helping students ground their conclusions in the concrete details they actually observe.

Students generated an impressive number of observations, inferences, and questions about the world depicted in the photograph. Significantly, there was a strong ethical component to their interpretations and conclusions (they want somebody to take responsibility for the conditions depicted), yet this rests upon a good amount of careful observation and background knowledge. As a framework, the photo-analysis guide helps teachers ask students for evidence for their views. If a student jumped to a conclusion such as "I think the boys killed the horse," for example, the teacher can ask, "Why? What do you observe in the picture that supports that?" In this way, while an exercise like this helps students locate what *they* find interesting and important in a topic, it *also* serves as a model of critical historical thinking. For historians no less than students, a "good" conclusion is one that is well supported by both evidence and background knowledge of the era.

On-line archives and their more open-ended materials, then, can crucially support the "messy" work of student interpretation, speculation, and forming hypotheses. The challenge for teachers is twofold: first, to let the mess happen—let students make wrong guesses, infer too much, draw simplistic conclusions; and second, to ask for evidence, to pose skeptical questions, to send them back to the sources, and to encourage the kinds of debate and thinking aloud through which students can refine their understanding of the problem. Because the focus is on thinking, the "messy" class-room is also the more rigorous one.

On-line Communication Forums

What are on-line communication forums, and how can they enrich the history classroom? There are two ways to understand the Web as a communication forum, one very broad, and the other more specific.

The World Wide Web

First, the Web itself, from the standpoint of a historian, can be viewed as a communication forum in which the meaning of historical events, figures, and ideas is constantly being negotiated by dozens of different constituencies. Second, there are growing numbers of public discussion forums about history that students can join, for brief or extended interactions. We will discuss both of these briefly, and provide a few examples.

Michael O'Malley and Roy Rosenzweig, two academic historians who have analyzed what the Web has to offer history teachers, have concluded that while the Web offers many exciting new resources, perhaps its most significant value lies in the way it demonstrates to students of history and culture how history is a living process, an ongoing conversation about the meaning of the past, framed by current needs and interests.[4] While the conversation is not always disciplined—one may find hobbyists and propagandists and hucksters weighing in as frequently as historians and thoughtful citizens—the Web nonetheless demonstrates the remarkable range and variety of contemporary uses of history. Further, understanding this variety can be a useful adjunct to helping students learn to distinguish a "disciplined" conversation about history from one that is undisciplined.

Teachers whose goal is to help students become more critical about the application of historical ideas in the present, then, may find the Web to be the ideal teaching medium. They will need to depart, however, from the common practice of "vetting" reliable or appropriate materials ahead of time. Instead, they will want to expose students to the full range of materials on the Web, and ask them to analyze and categorize them themselves. In doing so, it is important to recognize that using the Web to understand how history is actively *used* in contemporary culture is not the same as using it to learn about history. It is, however, a useful prelude or adjunct to that enterprise.

New Media in Action—Web Search Exercise: The Uses of History

Here is a simple exercise that models one way to introduce these critical, evaluative skills to students.

1) Have students conduct a Web search, using AltaVista or another major search engine, on a term or terms related to a common historical topic or figure. It is possible to choose topics that are somewhat controversial, such as the *Enola Gay*, the Battle of the Little Big Horn, Thomas Jefferson as a slaveholder, or the sixties counterculture. Part of the fun, however, can be finding that even the most staid or sedate of historical characters or topics can have very different meaning to different groups of people.

2) Ask students to locate a document with a strong or interesting point of view on the topic or figure, print it out, and summarize it according to questions such as these: What viewpoint is presented on the topic or person? What supporting evidence, if any, is provided? Who is the author and/or publisher of the document? To what group or category do they belong—scholars? hobbyists? governmental agency? advocacy group? commercial enterprise? private individual? What motives or interests might they have in relation to the topic?

3) Now ask students to find two or three documents that express a *different* point of view on the same historical figure or topic (it may be serious or lighthearted) and briefly summarize these in the same way. (This will take careful use of the search engine.)

4) Have students put together a brief presentation or written report describing the use and meaning of their historical figure or topic in contemporary culture. They will probably want to illustrate the different viewpoints expressed with images and quotations from the Web sites.

As one example, an AltaVista search on "Little Big Horn" yields the following documents among the first thirty hits:

◆ an oral history of the Battle of the Little Big Horn maintained by a western university;
◆ lyrics of a song titled "Little Big Horn" written and performed by a heavy-metal band;
◆ a site maintained by a group of military-history buffs who do reenactments of the battle;
◆ list-serv postings from a classroom teacher who explains why she believes teaching her students about the Battle of the Little Big Horn is important;
◆ a magazine reprint arguing that teaching about Native Americans has been hijacked by political correctness;
◆ materials maintained by the College of Little Big Horn, a ninety percent Native American college on a reservation in Montana;
◆ and an advertisement for the Little Big Horn Action Figure Playset, a collection of plastic children's toys.

Students can see that a single battle and its meaning and symbolism are marshaled by different interest groups for purposes that are educational, cultural, political, recreational, and commercial. A natural outcome of such an exercise is heightened interest in substantive historical questions, as students ask, "Well, what *really* happened?" They are now in a better position to frame their own questions on the topic and begin the task of deciding which of the resources they have found useful and reliable for their purposes. In sum, students doing research projects on virtually any historical topic or figure may benefit from looking at the varied ways these topics and characters are used, and abused, in contemporary culture.

On-line Discussions

A more specific kind of on-line communication forum that can enrich the history and social studies classroom is found in public discussion forums such as list servs, e-mail bulletin boards, and threaded conferencing systems. These can allow students to join in on the historical conversation, posing questions, offering opinions and interpretations, and debating issues.

Pedagogically, these forums widen the universe of discourse to which students are exposed, potentially helping them scaffold more sophisticated ways of building and communicating historical knowledge. It is possible, for example, for a high school student to talk about history with university scholars, elementary school students, irate taxpayers, elderly citizens with personal memory of events, and graduate students. Students may join these conversations for very specific purposes, or for more diffuse and extended interactions.

Three kinds of on-line discussion forums present themselves for students to join in on: 1) e-mail exchanges with scholars and other experts; 2) public discussions around broadcast media; and 3) special topic-based or "by-invitation" conversations on list servs and bulletin boards.

E-mail exchanges. At the most basic level, using e-mail alone, students can initiate conversations with university faculty, museum curators, and others who specialize in an area they are researching. While many such professionals will decline a student's invitation to such an exchange, many others will oblige, at least for short exchanges, and one or two out of every ten contacted may be willing to engage in an extended conversation. It is best if the teacher helps to establish the expectations surrounding an extended exchange, but students with access to the Internet and to e-mail can do the initial legwork.

One approach to locating faculty who may be willing to engage in e-mail exchanges is for students to use a standard search engine such as AltaVista, narrowing their search by including, along with topic words, the terms "research center" or "university" within quotation marks. It is not difficult to come up with four or five faculty e-mail addresses in this fashion. An even better approach is to use the "virtual libraries" maintained on many different topics by institutions of higher education around the world. An index of these virtual libraries can be found at http://www.vlib.org. Browsing within a topic such as "migration and immigration," students can find myriad scholars, government officials, curators, and other professionals to contact.

It is well to remember that from a media-literacy perspective as well as from common sense, teachers whose students get involved in e-mail exchanges with adults have a host of issues to teach about, all related to the special characteristics of e-mail as a semi-anonymous, non-synchronous yet potentially a very private and intimate form of communication. The risks and opportunities these features present for students of middle- and high-school age require that teachers help students establish expectations and boundaries for appropriate, respectful communication.

Public discussions around broadcast media. An increasing number of commercial and public broadcasting outlets are sponsoring on-line discussions of issues raised in their programming. These provide ideal vehicles for students to join in conversations around important topics that are also timely "media events," and as such may capture their interest at home as well as in school.

Large-scale public television productions such as Ken Burns's Civil War series, Ric Burns's *The West, Nova* science programs, *Frontline* documentaries, *POV* independent videos, and others, now often offer chances for viewers to go on-line and share their reactions to the programs. The programs' producers may or may not join in. Since students sometimes view these programs in conjunction with classroom study, joining in such larger discussions is a natural extension of classroom dialogue around a media experience. These on-line discussions should, however, follow within-class discussion.

It should be noted that commercial presenters of such programs as A&E Specials and children's programming such as *Wishbone* are increasingly moving toward making their Web sites more "active" spaces, allowing viewers to get additional material and offer reactions. These efforts, however, may have more to do with marketing than with stimulating genuine viewer discussion.

The premier place to go for access to public discussions around broadcast materials relating to history and social studies issues remains http://www.pbs.org. Teachers whose students join in on these kinds of public discussions will likely want to call students' attention to the options available to them (posing a question of their own, telling a story, responding to another post with agreement or disagreement, etc.). In order to cope with the strangely decontextualized kinds of conversation that occur in discussion groups (where little is said and much implied), teachers may also need to help students learn how to interpret clues to the discussants' perspectives and points of view. These include the domain and server names of URLs or e-mail addresses, which can indicate whether a discussant is working from a foreign or domestic university, business, technology group, or nonprofit organization.

Topic-based discussion groups. Electronic bulletin boards and list servs comprise the third kind of discussion forum that students can join. These are generally topic-based, and sometimes require participants to register as members before joining in. Students can profitably browse many lists and gain much from the conversation simply by reading, but the ideal forum enables students to jump right in. Again, the "virtual libraries" index (http://www.vlib.org), topically organized, is an ideal entry point for finding conversations on many history and social studies topics that are open to students.

As one example, a vlib bulletin board on the topic "immigration and migration" was queried by students asking for information about Irish immigration during the Industrial Revolution. This led to an exchange of twelve messages over two weeks, involving immigration scholars, lay people of Irish ancestry, and others. These kinds of forums have the advantage of reaching wide numbers of people, and getting answers only from those who are interested in responding to students; they are thus a good way of finding experts who may be willing to continue in e-mail conversation with teachers and students. Teachers using these forums will need to work with students around the protocols for communicating on-line, as in the forums above.

Composition and Publishing Tools

One feature of the "messy" history or social studies classroom is that students have many opportunities to formulate, express, and share what they are learning about history and social processes, and do so with varied audiences. They may keep a journal about their research, interview a grandparent and then annotate a family photo album, create a wall-sized timeline or other exhibit of their findings, or draft and illustrate a research monograph. Strictly speaking, new technologies are not required for this kind of composition and sharing, but they can help. A range of multimedia authoring tools offer support in the "messy" history classroom—desktop publishing programs, timeline makers, multimedia authoring programs that let students annotate images, and, of course, the Web itself (as an authoring environment). This discussion emphasizes only those composition tools that raise particularly interesting opportunities and challenges with respect to the goals of "messy" history: the ability to link the local and personal with the historical and national; the ability to represent historical complexity; the ability to interact with community members both as data and as audiences; and the ability to integrate narrative understanding with a critical stance toward sources. The definition of composition tools will be kept intentionally broad to address these different issues.

We will briefly discuss composition tools that allow and help students to do the following:

1) visualize historical change
2) personalize history
3) document and share local culture

Visualizing History: Timeline Makers

A relatively simple multimedia composition tool—the timeline maker—can be useful in helping students see patterns and complexity in historical change. Many teachers use programs such as Tom Snyder's *Timeliner* to print out custom time lines that fit the period they want, at the scale they want, and illustrated by icons of their own or their students' choosing. They find that using a time line as a frame of reference for historical study helps students get "the big picture"—the chronological ordering of events, and the ways that historians group events into eras, such as the twenties, or thirties, or the Great Depression. Students who make their *own* time lines, and use them as frameworks for representing what they are learning, can go several steps further. They can see how historical developments overlap and recur. They can see that historical "eras" are not natural, but are historians' constructions, and are defined not by one thing but by many, for example by distinctive types of work, leisure, politics, culture, and international relations. By mapping their own research findings onto the time line, they can understand something about the power and the limitations of historical periodization.

Take, for example, a recent eighth-grade class studying immigration in a New York City public school. As a small part of their unit of study, students, working in groups, created two large time lines on the walls of the classroom, one for the period 1880 to 1920 and one for the period 1980 to 2020. As they read about and discussed the world that turn-of-the-century immigrants to America encountered, students plotted terms for large-scale developments over the time line, including things like industrialization, immigration, urbanization, and concentration of wealth. Since the teacher had assigned each group a different aspect of turn-of-the-century life to research (work, amusement, transportation, cities and housing, national politics), she drew a line for each category underneath the timeline. As students gathered images, short texts, and statistics about their category, they occasionally selected artifacts to plot on the time line. This activity went on in the background of students' study, which was driven by an "essential question" about the experiences and impact of immigrants at the turn of the nineteenth century, and again at the turn of the twentieth century. After several weeks, students had filled an entire wall with material that made the big terms at the top of the time line—"industrialization" and "urbanization" for example—concrete and vivid, and suggested the interrelationships of economy, culture, and politics that makes any era distinctive. Students were able to speculate, for example, about connections between the factories that immigrants worked in and the wealth being amassed by industrialists, and between immigrants' difficult working and living conditions and the rise of movies and amusement parks (on the one hand) and labor unrest (on the other). Just as significant was the fact that students were now in a position to ask good questions about our own historical period. If people worked in factories then, where do they work now? What kinds of jobs do immigrants get? This led to discussion of the service jobs that have replaced what used to be mostly manufacturing jobs—for many teenagers as well as immigrants. How do people in these jobs feel about their work? Do they still go on strike if they are unhappy? What do they do for fun? How have amusements changed? Such question-posing helped prepare students for their research into immigrants' lives and jobs at the end of the twentieth century, which was conducted through interviews with recent immigrants, among other resources. This work yielded an equally interesting time line, and one that made clear that the future was if not wide open, at least uncertain.

Personalizing History: Genealogy Makers

Doing a family history project is justly a part of most students' school experience. After all, knowing our own family's history, understanding where we have come from, is one of the most important ways that we locate ourselves in the present and give meaning and direction to our lives. Knowing our own family history also helps us build a larger and more coherent story of the society and culture of which we are a part. Genealogy makers are useful tools in planning, gathering, and representing family history information that students gather when undertaking a family history project. A good program, such as *Family Tree Maker* (Broderbund Software, 1998), enables students to create and revise family tree diagrams, and easily input, link, and later access text, audio, and visual information about family members' experiences through time. An exceptional program enables students to link a single family's experiences to larger historical events and circumstances, showing connections between these events and their own family's or other families' lives. Composing such a multimedia document can reinforce students' ability to see history as a human struggle of people much like themselves, and, indeed, their ability to see history as intimately connected to their own lives.

One such program, created as a prototype by teachers at the Bank Street School for Children, is called *Family Stories*. The program lets students "create" a family, real or fictional, over several generations. Bank Street teachers choose to have twelve-year-old students create fictional families, since by this age they have done histories of their own families and the teachers want them to stretch further, to the study of nineteenth-century immigrants, or African American history, or Asian cultures.

Students start by creating a genealogy in the familiar form of a family tree. They place the family tree in a historical context by aligning it next to a timeline. Symbols on the time line represent historical events that are described in a text created by the teacher (or the student). The computer makes it easy to move, align, and link these icons to represent relationships. Students link their family trees to a virtual "scrapbook" of artifacts they have carefully chosen and modified from on-line libraries to tell the story of the family through time. These include letters, diary entries, photographs, newspaper clippings, birth, marriage, and death certificates, work and school documents, and images of home and neighborhood.

To create their fictional family albums, students need to ask themselves "What might have happened to this kind of family during this period in that place?" Students at Bank Street are given clear parameters. They are assigned families of particular ethnic backgrounds, given secondary works to read on the group, and told they must chronicle certain time spans and certain basic life experiences, such as immigration or slavery. Still, it is up to the students to decide whether and how historical events such as the Civil War, or the invention of the automobile, or the Depression, will appear in the lives of particular family members. As they assemble and create artifacts to tell their family's story, they quickly confront the challenge of making their fictional accounts historically accurate. That is, they must invent names, choose portraits, artifacts, and other documents, and describe details of income and social behavior that fit into the historical period and the social group they are representing. A key role of teachers is to point out anachronisms and encourage students to conduct further research and revisions.

Students invest great imagination in their family stories, inventing dramas of achievement, love, and loss worthy of great melodrama. Encouraged by teachers, they also invest great care in making their narratives historically accurate.

Teachers report that students have a deeper and richer understanding of a topic like immigration after creating these genealogies, in several ways. First, they have a greater sense of the material culture of the time period, since they have had to research, illustrate, and describe the details of how people actually

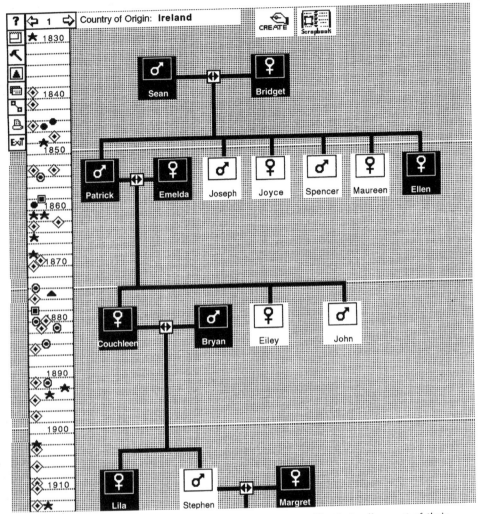

Screen shot: Students construct a hypothetical immigrant "family tree" as part of their study of immigration. (From *Family Stories,* a set of software tools created by Stan Brimberg and Diana Granat of the Bank Street School for Children, 1993.)

lived, with what technologies, with what clothing and architecture, and so on. Second, they have had a more human and personal understanding of the historical events, having imagined them through the eyes of characters they care about. (Students in Bank Street classes have consistently wished to "act out" their family story while presenting it to the class.) Finally, they are more savvy about the perils of historical representation. Having seen how easy it is to "doctor" a photograph, or use a document

| McGuire |
| A letter from an Irish friend |

Link ⏎ ◁ 2 0 ▷ CREATE

> Dear Margaret,
>   June 7,
> 1926
>
>   How are you? It has finally come to the point where I have
> decided I can not live in Ireland anymore! Now that there is the
> Republic of Ireland, I now have more opportunities. I have
> decided to find those in the U.S. who will pay me for my labor. I am
> coming over to America. I will be working as an indentured
> servant, a maid for the Churchills. I will live with them also. They
> seem to be a nice family. They are very wealthy, and live
> extravagantly. I have to work for them for seven years. I hope my
> experience with them will be pleasant.
>
>   I have heard much good news about it from your mother's
> letters she sent last month. It sounds like I could easily find an
> unskilled labor job right away.
>
>   I'll see you soon, Margret, and give my love to Stephen.
>   Love always, Erin M

Screen shot: Students annotate their family tree by creating "scrapbook" artifacts that tell the family's story through time.

from the twentieth century in place of what should be a nine-teenth-century document, students are more likely, according to teachers, to be critical of other historical accounts.

Documenting and Sharing Local Culture

Young people living in Appalachia videotape local folk artists in order to counter media stereotypes of ignorant, impoverished Appalachians. In the aftermath of racial rioting, African American and Latino teens in New York City make a video about the complex history of cooperation between African Americans and American Jews. Youngsters in Washington, D.C., create and annotate photo portraits of their urban neighborhoods in order to challenge the despair that often prevails among teachers, social workers, and other adults around them.

In these and other projects, video camcorders (and plain old cameras) are being used by students to compose and share the histories of their own communities, and from their own perspectives. At the Educational Video Center in New York City, high school students work in groups to research, shoot, edit, and screen independent video documentaries about social and historical topics of importance to them and their communities. Historical topics have included the civil rights struggles of the 1960s, African American–Jewish relations, and the history of media stereotyping.

Video documentary is a natural adjunct to the active and "messy" history and social studies classroom. It is worthwhile to consider how the video medium supports and enables classroom inquiry into historical and social topics. A camcorder enables students to leave the confines of the classroom and strictly academic resources, and go out and capture authentic pieces of the community and their social world. The lens brings those pieces of the world—oral histories with community members, the social spaces of the street and the neighborhood, people's arguments and opinions about controversial topics—up close, and allows students to put them under a microscope for dissection and study. The archive of videotapes now available at any rental outlet also means that students can draw on a wide variety of historical imagery in their work, linking contemporary images of people, communities, and social problems to their representation in earlier eras. The video editor enables students to stitch these pieces together, along with their own written narration, into an argument of their own. Finally, the ubiquitous VCR and the popularity of video enable students to share their work with diverse audiences, gather reactions, and lead discussions. In cases where the students have documented a local population or culture, such as senior citizens in a nursing home, or local folk artists, the video work may have great importance for the community as one of few lasting records.

Typically, however, video production is not used as an adjunct to in-depth classroom and community-based learning about a vital topic or issue. More often students are given camcorders in order to document a school event, or to learn technical and vocational skills, or simply as an alternative to traditional media for doing reports, as a new way to "express themselves."

New Media in Action—Video Production as Inquiry:
The Writing-Process Analogy

One way for teachers who are not familiar with video production to understand how it can be organized to promote classroom inquiry is to use an analogy to the writing process. At a very general level, professional video production corresponds to the broad stages of the writing process, including planning (preproduction), writing (production), and revising and editing (postproduction). On a more specific level, common features of the writing-process approach include immersion in literature, free-writing, finding a topic, writing multiple drafts and sharing them with peers, and polishing a finished piece. In a similar way, teachers can guide students through a video-production process that includes immersion in video genres, free exploration with the camera, choosing and researching topics, shooting and logging footage, editing and screening rough cuts to peers and others, and reediting the final version.

Each of the following key moments in EVC's production process suggests, by way of analogy to the writing process, ways for classroom teachers to deepen their students' work with video production.

A) Immersion in video genres. Just as all good writers are readers first, so video makers must be viewers first. In order for the students to become familiar with the documentary genre, the video workshop at EVC begins with a screening of a range of works, including those made by youth producers and people of different cultural backgrounds. Following each, students write about and discuss the makers' intentions, the target audiences, and stylistic differences. They begin to see that the communicative range of video is wider than simply mainstream television and MTV, and to understand the values and conventions that distinguish the independent documentary genre. For example, the following exchange took place after students watched a segment of the historical documentary *Eyes on the Prize*:

PAM (*instructor*): *You've said that documentaries are about truth and facts. What do you think the filmmaker's purpose here was?*

DANNETTE (*seventeen*): *To show how racism affected those people, and how they changed things.*

TROY *(eighteen): The guy who did it did a good job.*

PAM: Why?

TROY: *Because it got me upset. It makes me want to fight.*

PAM: *So it had an emotional effect. Is that what a documentary should do?*

DAPHNE *(seventeen): Yes. But then some people might get angry at the documentary instead of at the things it showed.*

B) First camera workshop. The point of free-writing is to write without inhibitions or worrying about mistakes in order to "get comfortable" with one's materials. Students' initial work with the camera can be organized in a similar way. At EVC, students work in small groups to set up and experiment with the features of the camera, without worrying unduly about the outcome. They may shoot mock interviews, for example, in a "man on the street" or talk show format. The point is to "get a feel" for setting up and handling sometimes awkward equipment, and to note how changes in lighting, framing, camera angle, and movement influence how the subject appears.

We observed that students' initial choices in relation to the equipment often said something about their past experiences with media, as when girls shied away from the camera or particular boys kept on "hamming it up." In the classroom, teachers can encourage students to rotate through different roles so that everyone has a chance to work the camera, monitor sound, act as "talent," or be the director, for example.

C) Choosing a topic. A critical step in any composition process, finding a topic that matters to *all* students is even more important in the video medium, since success depends on the commitment of every member of the production team. At EVC, choosing topics is an intensive two-day process that begins with brainstorming and exploratory writing in order to generate a long list of issues that deeply concern students. The second day, students draft mini-proposals for the topics most important to them and argue for them before the group until less workable topics are gradually eliminated. Instructors suggest the following questions as criteria: Is the topic important to a youth audience? Will it provoke all viewers to think and respond? Is it practical to do in the time and with the resources and contacts that we have? Which would you most like to work on? Students are asked to envision what a tape on their topic might look like and list the kinds of images and sounds that might be necessary to realize it.

Classroom teachers can adapt this process in a number of ways, substituting criteria that reflect their goals for students. The result should be a topic that all students feel genuinely interested in pursuing.

D) Research and planning. At EVC, research begins with students generating an initial set of questions they need to find answers to. Next, they brainstorm all the possible resources, locations, and personal contacts that might serve as sources of useful information. They are encouraged to consider their own neighbors, friends, and family members as potential resources, in addition to more "official" sources. Teams then choose which questions and which resources they will investigate. Some may head for the phones, some for the library, others out to scout locations. They share what they have discovered in daily production conferences, a structure analogous to the "writing conference" that allows instructors to help students refine their questions as they plan for interviews and location shoots.

E) Shooting and logging footage. Shoots provide opportunities for students to perform one of several creative roles: camera, sound recorder, interviewer, script person, and director, to name a few. At EVC, roles are decided on ahead of time so that students can practice if necessary. Each role offers its own challenges, risks, and rewards. Interviewers, for example, need to be prepared to ask follow-up questions in order to get what they need from their subjects. The camera person must maintain focus, steadiness, and good framing, and try to anticipate "where the action is" visually. A director must act as a leader who can keep the team focused on getting the best images and sounds possible within the constraints of the shoot.

Promptly screening raw footage with the group and discussing what its strengths and weaknesses are nonjudgmentally is one way that EVC helps students understand good production techniques. In logging the tapes, and methodically summarizing all the video and audio shot, students gain an invaluable familiarity with the material they will shape into a coherent story.

F) Editing and sharing rough cuts. The editing phase is where students draw together all the materials they have gathered, along with their complex feelings about the issue, in order to build their own argument. The process starts with the building of an edit plan, a rough outline of the tape's main ideas and the images, sounds, and interviews that will convey them. Instructors at EVC encourage students to think more visually at this stage as they begin to design the form as well as the content of the tape. One or two "rough-cut" versions of the videotape, analogous to writing drafts, are then edited, and can be screened to different audiences.

G) Public screening of final tape. Public screenings allow youngsters to connect with real audiences for their work. At EVC, effort is made to have the audience for the final screening as diverse as possible, including parents, peers, teachers, media professionals, and community members. At the screening, students briefly introduce their tape, and afterward preside over the lively debate that tapes inevitably provoke. The atmosphere is usually both serious and celebratory. Students feel obvious pride in what they have accomplished and the considerable effort that went into it, but also feel compelled to address the audience's questions, often in great depth. In schools, screenings and discussions can occur with groups of peers, teachers, and/or parents. Where their content is appropriate for younger students, the tapes can be used by students for peer-teaching.

Student video production, on the inquiry model suggested here, is an ambitious undertaking. It requires that teachers use the production process itself to organize learning over a significant period of time. Teachers need many kinds of institutional support for this kind of curriculum change, including more preparation time, longer class periods, access to equipment and technical support, the ability to purchase supplies (such as batteries or cables) on short notice, and freedom to leave the school building with students and equipment. In addition, this model may mean relinquishing control over much of the learning process to students, since few teachers are proficient in the video medium.

Historical Simulations

In discussing the first three genres of new media—on-line archives, discussion forums, and composition tools—we have emphasized ways of using these tools to help students develop a more personal stake in history, to dig actively and imaginatively into the past, and to relate it to their lives outside of school. To develop a personal interest in historical thinking and discourse is to recognize that all history is, to some extent, subjective.

When students role-play a historical character, interpret a primary document, witness arguments among historians, and document their own family and local history, they are learning that history, while based on evidence, exists through interpretation. The fact that all historical accounts are partial accounts—that they are based on incomplete and fragmentary evidence, and that they reflect something of their authors' points of view—calls for a kind of critical approach to history that is much the same as being media literate. In both cases the savvy learner needs to ask: Whose account is this? What is their point of view? What is the evidence behind it? Is there other evidence I can bring to bear? What else is this connected to? Why, and to whom, does this matter? Thus, as students use media tools to develop a more critical sense of the past, teachers and students should reflect on the ways the media tools they use may themselves be shaping and framing the historical knowledge they build.

Students and teachers alike love successful simulations. Simulations put students in the role of real people doing real activities. Because of this they fit nicely into an active-learning pedagogy. Simulations can be educationally powerful because they invoke young people's yearning to role-play, to imagine themselves as grown-up, and to try out possible selves. They set up a world of "as if" in which students can invest not only their minds but their imaginations as well.

Simulations are different from role-playing and drama exercises, however, in that in simulations there are rules and formulas that determine "what happens" when a person or group makes a particular decision. These rules are a necessary part of simulations, whether they are embodied in printed worksheets, in board games, or in computer-based programs. Yet every system of rules that purports to be *like* the real world in some ways is in very many more ways *un*like the world.

Simulations, after all, are essentially simplifications of reality. They are designed to highlight, for educational and recreational purposes, a few relatively systematic properties of the world. To do this they suppress all the "noise" and contingency that inevitably characterize the real world. Every author of a simulation faces certain choices—which elements of reality to highlight, how systematic to make them appear, and what to leave out. These choices embody a whole variety of assumptions about the way the world works or ought to work, as well as value judgments about the worth of people, objects, and ideas.

The assumptions and value judgments at the root of any simulation are often masked, however, by the "reality principle" of the simulation—the feeling the simulation gives to players that they are immersed in a "real" world. In the classroom, then, it may be important, after students have been immersed in the simulation's "reality," to revisit the rules of the game and to explicitly examine the assumptions on which the reality has been based.

Technology-based simulations make the challenge of finding the simulation's "reality" even more difficult, for two reasons. First, they often present the world with great verisimilitude. Pictures, graphics, animation, sound, and especially real-time responsiveness help users forget they are in a game. Second, they are often based on sophisticated algorithms that model physical, economic, and social processes in very complex ways, so that it is hard for users to feel that they are *not* reality.

To become more literate about simulations and their uses (and abuses), students should be given opportunities to revisit a simulation after they have played it and consider these general questions:

♦ What did you learn (from manipulating this part of the simulation)?
♦ What aspects or qualities of the "real world" were left out of the simulation?
♦ How could the model of the real world presented by the simulation be different? What could you put in to make it more realistic?

What follows is a description of how a popular historical simulation, *The Oregon Trail* (MECC, 1996), can be used to enliven students' understanding of the American West. It also illustrates how classroom discussion based on the questions above can, in turn, raise questions about the adequacy of the simulation, and provide materials for further investigations. While this activity is specific to *The Oregon Trail*, the approach can be extended to any social studies or historical simulation used in the middle- or high-school classroom.

New Media in Action—Media Literacy Activity: The Oregon Trail Examining the Rules of the Game

Overview

This exercise is intended to help students evaluate the rules and assumptions underlying a computer-based simulation, comparing these to information derived from other reference works and their own experience.

Objectives

Students will be able to:

◆ Describe what a simulation is, with an example, and explain its value;
◆ Describe the ways in which a particular simulation (e.g., *The Oregon Trail*) is faithful to the reality it depicts, and the ways in which it simplifies reality;
◆ Be able to suggest modifications to a simulation to make it more realistic.

Prior Activities

All students should have played *The Oregon Trail* prior to the activity. Play may be in the form of a game (i.e., without the teacher having independent learning goals for students), or as part of a focused activity, such as those suggested in the Teacher Guide distributed by MECC, the program publisher.

Exercises

1. Examining the options in "Choosing Occupations"

A. Ask students to share their occupational choices and explain why they chose the occupation they did. (You can print out the chart above or list the occupations on the board.) Which occupations do they think are best? Which worst? Why? How do they know?

B. Ask students to look carefully at the chart Occupation Help below. It shows the "value" the simulation attaches to each occupation. (Note that good simulations enable you to view the underlying mathematical model in this way. *Very* good simulations enable you to *modify* the mathematical model.)

In this chart students can see that there is a neat inverse relationship between the amount of cash that a given occupation confers and the "bonus" score given each occupation (which is computed at the game's end, and which may be interpreted as the long-term or "social value" of the occupation). In between are the "special advantages" that enable selected occupations to respond to crises that occur on the trail.

Name: _____

Occupation
- ● Banker
- ○ Blacksmith
- ○ Carpenter
- ○ Doctor
- ○ Farmer
- ○ Merchant
- ○ Saddlemaker
- ○ Teacher

HELP

The other people in your wagon:
| Emily |
| Jed |
| Sara |
| Joey |

OK

Screen shot: Choosing occupations in *The Oregon Trail*.

Occupation Help

People from all walks of life went west to Oregon. You can pick your occupation, but each choice has its advantages and disadvantages.

Occupation	Starting Cash	Special Advantages	Final Bonus
Bankers	$ 1,600	none	none
Doctors	1,200	sick or injured people are less likely to die	none
Merchants	1,200	none	x 1.5
Blacksmiths	800	more likely to repair broken wagon parts	x 2
Carpenters	800	more likely to repair broken wagon parts	x 2
Saddlemakers	800	none	x 2.5
Farmers	400	oxen are less likely to get sick and die	x 3
Teachers	400	none	x 3.5

OK

Screen shot: *The Oregon Trail.*

C. Hold a class discussion aimed at evaluating the "worth" of the occupations from the perspective of the program, and from students' own perspectives. The following questions may assist in focusing discussion:

♦ According to the program, which are the best occupations? Worst?

♦ Why do teachers have the highest bonus points and doctors none?

♦ What occupations are left out, and why (child care, artist, prostitute)?

♦ Could the occupational choices be made more realistic or complete? How?

2. Comparing information from other sources

A. Based on their experience playing the program, have students summarize the simulation's treatment of one of the following topics, or others:

♦ Emigrants' relations with Native Americans

♦ The experience of women pioneers vs. men pioneers

♦ Emigrants' decisions to continue, stop, or turn back

B. Have students read about the same topic in one of the

following resources about the westward migration (or others found, for example, in the library or on the World Wide Web):

DeVoto, Bernard. *Across the Wide Missouri.* Reprint. New York: American Legacy Press, 1947.

Schlissel, Lillian. *Women's Diaries of the Westward Journey.* New York: Schocken Books, 1982.

Worcester, Don, ed. *Pioneer Trails West.* Caldwell, Idaho: Caxton Printers, Ltd., 1985.

C. Ask students to prepare a brief presentation or written report that summarizes what they have read about the topic and compares the simulation's treatment of it. The following questions may help guide the comparison:

- ◆ What historical experiences were included in the simulation?
- ◆ Which were left out? Why? Do you think this is a good reason?
- ◆ How could the simulation be changed to reflect the information you have found?

3. Comparing the simulation to your own experience

A. Have students write about their character's experience of death and dying during the game. Who died? In what order? How did it "feel" to you as a player when this happened?

B. Ask students to write about what it might have actually felt like to be a pioneer and have a friend or loved one die while on the trail with you. Note: You might assign as background reading a first-person account of this kind of experience, such as *Narcissa Whitman on the Oregon Trail* by Lawrence Dodd (Washington: Ye Galleon Press, 1985).

C. Hold a class discussion about the role of death and dying in computer games and simulations. Is a simulation or game-maker "wrong" for treating death in this way? Why or why not? Would you want to change this aspect of it? How?

◆ Conclusion: Using Media to Develop a Rich and Critical Sense of the Past

In this chapter we have surveyed several genres of new media that can serve good history and social studies teaching and suggested how they may be used critically in the history classroom. We have seen how on-line archives offer students the chance to do history actively, building their own historical knowledge from vastly richer and more varied bodies of primary-source materials. We have considered how on-line conversation forums enable students to enter ongoing cultural dialogues about the meaning of historical events and figures. We have noted the power of composition and publishing tools in helping students construct and share a deeper and more personal understanding of history with a variety of audiences. And we have highlighted the ability of historical simulations to invoke students' imaginative identification with characters and settings that are distant in time while at the same time underscoring the need for students and teachers to reflect on what may be missing from such simulations.

In concluding, it is worth noting how these issues of media in the changed (more messy, more democratic) history and social studies classroom are connected to the larger social history of media in western societies. At least since the invention of the printing press, the development and use of media has been a site of constant struggle between those with social power and privilege and those without them, as one social group after another has sought the ability to read and speak in the dominant medium, and has thereby changed both the medium and the conditions of social life.

Scholars who have studied the growing democratization of American society during the nineteenth and early twentieth centuries have noted that it was supported by an unprecedented expansion of print literacy among workingpeople, African Americans, immigrants, women, and the poor. They have gone on to suggest that a key dynamic of this democratization was the ability of each group, using the tools of linguistic media, to create a place for itself, and for its own particular history, within the larger argument about the future of American democracy. Now, near the close of the twentieth century, the image has become the prime means of public address by the powerful, while the printed word, though not in complete decline, seems at least to be increasingly marginalized.

It may not be a coincidence, then, that American culture is marked by a peculiar form of historical amnesia—a present-orientation that treats the past as nostalgia rather than as a dynamic resource for building a more just and democratic society. Most troubling is the fact that those most in need of historical awareness are those most often denied it, as public schools continue to struggle to provide little more than the most basic literacy to students with the fewest social and economic opportunities. Viewed in this context, the task of helping all students use media tools to creatively recover a rich, synthetic, and critical sense of the past takes on a new kind of urgency.

NOTES

1. D. Ravitch and C. Finn, *What Do Our 17-Year Olds Know? A Report on the First National Assessment of History and Literature.* New York: Harper & Row, 1987.

2. National Council for History Education. "Reinvigorating History in U.S. Schools: Reform Recommendations for the States." http://www.history.org/nche. See also National Center for History in the Schools. *National Standards for United States History.* Los Angeles: University of California at Los Angeles, 1996.

3. M. O'Malley and R. Rosenzweig. "Brave New World or Blind Alley? American History on the World Wide Web." *The Journal of American History,* June 1997, pp. 132–155.

4. Ibid.

· 4 ·

Arts Education and the New Media

◆ **Standards-based Arts Education and the New Media**

The goals of successful art education programs are defined in the National Standards for Arts Education in a document prepared by the Consortium of National Arts Education Associations in 1994 and endorsed by a wide range of arts and educational organizations. New York City has its own curriculum frameworks based on those standards. Arts teachers everywhere are trying to develop curricula that support those standards and that help their students achieve the kind of relationship to arts articulated in them.

How can new technology support the challenging and imaginative arts curricula implied by the standards? In this chapter we focus on the visual arts and consider how the new media can be used to support the kind of arts education represented in the national standards.

Categories of Arts Education

There are many ways to categorize the major components to arts education. The New York City arts education standards define four areas:

- Creating, performing, and participating in the arts
- Knowing and using arts materials and resources
- Responding to and analyzing works of art
- Understanding the cultural dimensions and contributions of the arts.
  (*Curriculum Frameworks-Grades Pre-K–12* ©1995 The Board of Education of the City of New York)

A more traditional way to categorize the elements of arts education is to talk about *art history, art appreciation,* and *studio art.*

In this way of defining arts education, studio art is equivalent to creating and participating in the arts, knowing and using arts materials and resources as its focus. Art history is about understanding the cultural dimensions and contributions of the arts. Art appreciation is analogous to the ability to respond to and analyze works of art. The purpose of this chapter is to describe some ways each of these aspects of arts education can be supported through a media-literate use of the new digital technologies in accordance with the kind of hands-on education implied in the standards.

New Media and the Art Experience

Computer art is a rich, interesting, powerful, accessible medium in which artists are learning to express new ideas in new ways.

New Tools and New Opportunities

Multimedia computers are also an increasingly important part of the "tool kit" many artists use to do their work, whether engaged in commercial art or fine arts. Studio arts, then, can include learning to make art with computers and the peripheral technologies and applications, from scanners to printers, from desktop publishing to Web design. The new medium also provides opportunities to collaborate in ongoing on-line art projects that span time and space and to exhibit student work in new ways to new audiences.

Access and Exploration

For learning about artistic tradition, about the contributions various cultures have made to our common artistic heritage and about the different roles art and artists have played in the development of cultures, the new media bring an enormous wealth of resources, from virtual museums to conversations with living artists about their work. The new digital availability of such art treasures and conversations about art promises possibilities for art education, but it does not by itself constitute genuine access.

To make such resources accessible to students, they have to be identified, located, and evaluated, and a meaningful context for them has to be provided by the assignment and activities designed by teachers. It makes no more pedagogical sense to send students out into a virtual museum without a good assignment than it does to send them into a real museum without preparation or follow-up. Students will get no more out of overhearing a conversation among artists in a virtual space than they would out of listening to such a conversation in a real café. On-line artists are no more articulate about their work and no more able to address the kinds of concerns students have than other types of artists. Some are wonderful at talking and working with students, some communicate only through their work. Teachers still have to prepare the ground, guide the interpretation of the events, and make sure all their students get a chance to learn what they need.

Examples and Analytical Tools

For the art appreciation aspect of arts education, the new media provide both a rich set of examples to investigate and a new set of analytical tools. In some ways the new media allow art teachers to make all their constructivist dreams come true. It is now possible to take a work of art apart, examine it in detail, put it back together in different ways to study its form, its composition, its tone, and its feel by manipulating its elements—without ever losing sight of the original construction. The medium allows us to hold a moving object still to investigate it, by examining any frame of a film, for instance, and comparing it at will with any other frame. It also allows us to set a still object in motion, as it were, by altering its shape, size, colors, texture, or placement.

This increased ability to play with the object, to alter it in order to understand it, to compare and contrast it, to take it out of one context and place it into another, or to provide easy, instant, inviting links to contextual information about the object makes the medium particularly interesting for art appreciation or aesthetic literacy education. The digital, noncorporeal, abstract nature of the medium, the ease with which students can examine complex images, take them apart, turn them over, and reconstitute them can help them learn to see more and to derive a deeper, more informed pleasure from what they see.

Pleasure

And, finally, there is pleasure. There is a generation gap when it comes to perceiving these new media as a source of pleasure. Many adults who derive great enjoyment from the feel of a new book, from a visit to a quiet, well-lit museum, from a classical concert or a dance performance or from a thought-provoking evening at the theater consider the new media merely mindless entertainment. Some may admit that some films deserve the name of art, but they would find it difficult to grant a rock concert or a video game the same status. And yet so many of their children, students, and younger friends and colleagues derive deep, lasting pleasure from listening to their favorite rock bands or playing a visually exciting and imaginatively stimulating video game. It is true that most rock music is not very complex and most video games are based on very simplistic story lines and a lot of repetitive action, but the pleasures they bring are real enough.

If the life-long ability to enjoy the arts, to perceive ourselves more deeply through them, and to enhance the quality of our lives is truly one of the main goals of arts education, then the pleasures brought by the new media have to be taken seriously. For instance, spending many hours wandering through the dreamlike, gorgeous landscape of *Myst* or *Riven* (its even more beautiful sequel) can be as powerful an aesthetic experience as any museum visit or concert. Not only is there a great deal to see and to hear, but there is all that meaning-making going on. Playing the game means trying to understand the landscape, interpreting its objects and vistas, deciphering its culture. The clues are primarily visual and auditory. You have to make sense of why things look and sound the way they do. You have to focus on design and story line, on the relationship between form and function. Whether you succeed in coming up with an interpretation that unlocks all the secrets of this virtual universe or not, the activity itself is one of deep aesthetic (as well as intellectual) pleasure.

The new media offer opportunities for opening the pleasures of art to new audiences. A lot of students who do not think of themselves as artists or as interested in art would love to make a music video or a computer game to express their feelings about their music or their world.

In the last part of this chapter we look in depth at some questions students might learn to ask of interactive art resources as a basis for developing appropriate criteria for evaluating them. First, however, let us take a more general look at the kinds of new media resources currently available in the educational world, and how they might support standards-based arts education.

New Media and Studio Art

What the New Media Contribute

The arts standards focus on sharpening students' abilities to perceive the world around them and on allowing them to express their deepest insights about that world and their own role in it. The New York City standards stress that the arts nurture multiple intelligences and are thus important in developing such abilities as independent risk taking, harmonious collaboration, imaginative problem solving, and effective communication. They also point out that the arts foster discipline, concentration, creativity, intuition, and logic.

In the context of studio art, the new technologies provide a new medium and new tools for making art. Photography was once a new medium that was not readily accepted as art. Now it is taught in many arts programs, and it seems obvious that both the technical knowledge and the artistic vision required to compose and edit photographic images belong within the domain of visual arts education. The new media bring digital images, still and moving, within the domain of arts education. In a good art classroom, students are exposed to a wealth of different media. Sometimes they are asked to use a particular medium to express an idea, sometimes they are invited to choose a medium that is best suited to the idea they wish to express. They come to learn not only how to use the medium but also the strengths of different media, the ways in which the medium itself affects what an artist can do. They learn to explore the media and to use them judiciously and effectively for expressive and communicative purposes. In this context, digital images are particularly interesting.

What Skills Are Needed?

Some of the technical skills or talents required to compose complex images, animations, or multimedia installations are different from the kinds of skills or talents students often associate with being "good at art," and some are the same or similar. You don't have to know how to draw accurately to compose a digital image. You do have to have a "good eye" to compose such an image as well as patience to do it again and again until it looks right. You have to be willing to persist to overcome technical limitations, and to have the discipline to save the image so it does not disappear. Of course, patience and a "good eye" are as important for a paper collage as for a digital image, but the problem of saving the work is somewhat different, if only in degree. Many art media require careful tending. Clay can dry out, oil paint can smudge, paper can tear. Digital work can disappear if it is not properly stored. There are other technical skills required to take full advantage of the digital medium, including programming interactivity.

Working with Interactive Media

The digital medium is enormously flexible and powerful, but it lacks the warmth of something tangible and available to the senses in a variety of ways. What gives the medium its special quality, what makes up for its coldness, is its responsiveness. The equivalent of warmth comes from the extent to which one can interact with a digital work—engage in a kind of conversation with it by playing with it, experiencing it from different points of view depending on one's own pleasures and desires—the extent, in other words, to which it responds directly to our engagement with it. Figuring out not only how to represent an idea or express a feeling but also how to design this kind of conversation between the work and its audience fosters all the skills defined in the arts education standards.

In a sense, the digital medium is more like theater than like photography or painting in that it often requires collaboration among students with very different talents and interests. In making an interactive multimedia installation, for instance, one student may bring graphic talents to the endeavor and design the look of the work. Another might be good at research and planning and organize the search for material or the flow of production. Another might be a talented programmer, particularly good at figuring out how to make the program interact with audiences in a way that fits the ideas expressed in it.

Who and Where Is the Audience?

Getting these programs "right" is important to some students because these works have such a vast potential audience. They can be seen or interacted with by people across time and space if they are published on the Internet, for instance, or can exist in software libraries to be downloaded and viewed by anyone at any time. This raises the ante on the production. It makes collaboration more tense, more complicated. Values conflicts among collaborators, differences in taste, interpretation, goals, or acceptable standards of excellence can no longer simply be resolved by "psyching out" what the teacher wants. The fact that these works represent the students to the world (and not just to the teacher and the class) can exacerbate existing tensions and create new hierarchies.

Opportunities for Collaboration

It's possible that the very students who may have opted out of work with traditional media but whose imaginations might have started to flower with these media will end up silenced again or relegated to the status of "behind the scenes" contributors. On the other hand, the very same pressure, the potential of a real audience, also helps students face these kinds of tensions and motivates them to learn how to become more harmonious in their collaboration because something real is at stake for them. In many media projects, students mention collaboration as the most important thing they have learned.

New Conventions

There are few established conventions for making interactive multimedia programs. When Apple Computer first released *Hypercard* with every Macintosh, many people started to make stacks in which a little house icon meant "go to the table of contents," a bent arrow meant "retrace your step," an arrow pointing to the right meant "go to the next card in this sequence," and an arrow pointing to the left meant "previous card in this sequence." In a similar way, tabs across the top or down the left side of a Web site are becoming a convention. They allow readers to go directly to the first page of each section from anywhere in the document. These are new conventions. Because the medium is so new, students have a genuine opportunity to invent such conventions. This requires a particular kind of risk-taking, where students are responsible for inventing the form even as they explore it.

Taking Risks

There is another kind of risk-taking involved here too. An interactive program can fail far more dramatically than a painting. When it does not work right, it is no good. This is not a matter of taste but of faulty design. The images may be interesting and inviting, but if nothing happens when you try to interact with them, if you get lost trying to navigate through the work, or if it crashes the system, the experience is unsatisfying. On the other hand, the programming may be brilliant and inventive, and you may be able to zip back and forth among images and texts and sounds, but if none of the content is interesting, the experience feels empty. When peers deem a multimedia interactive "cool," it is because it was fun to play with *and* it looked good *and* it made some kind of sense. Developing age-appropriate criteria for assessing such productions is one of the things students and teachers have to invent together.

Problem-solving

The very richness of the medium—the fact that you can use sounds, images, texts, movies, voices, music, animations, and interactions with data, with people, and with the very stuff of the work itself—requires a great deal of imaginative problem-solving. If you can represent any thing in any way, then choices become central. For most students, however, it is less a matter of choice than a matter of stretching their relatively limited technical resources and skills to encompass their vision. It is the negotiation between what they imagine and what they can actually do that provides so many opportunities for creative problem-solving. This back-and-forth between the vision and the constraints of the medium is central to all arts education. In this new medium there's no long history of ways others have solved problems successfully. And the technology is changing so rapidly that any given set of procedures or tools will probably be obsolete tomorrow.

Everybody is figuring out whether it can be done and how to do it. Some things are technically simple, but it's hard to tell how meaningful they will remain over time. The point is that there is as yet no tradition, no authority in this medium. We don't yet know how to determine whether a digital work has "lasting artistic value." What matters most at this point is whether any given piece of work manages to communicate satisfactorily to some particular target audience.

Communicating Through and About Art

This emphasis on communication rather than on a more abstract notion of aesthetic quality, like "truth" or "beauty," is very useful in an educational setting. Students like and need to communicate with their peers and with their parents. Rather than simply reflecting adult tastes and criteria, they can invent their own. This is a benefit, however, only if they learn how to determine whether the communication has been effective. That means learning how to talk about the aesthetic experience with others, to articulate how art makes them feel and think, to listen to others, and to relate what others experience to the structure of the work itself— that is, to the decisions they made as they were creating it.

New Tools

Before we can discuss the work, however, we have to make it. The new media provide an amazing set of composition tools. There are any number of good graphics programs for needs ranging from young children's to professionals'. Of course, painting with electronic tools is no substitute for the sensual quality of painting with brushes or drawing with crayons. The electronic "place" where the images come together does not "feel" or respond like paper or canvas. But the ability to design stories and illustrate them with collages made from stamps and visual effects, hand-drawn shapes, and homemade sounds is very powerful. The medium allows some students, especially those with physical challenges to overcome, to express themselves in new and welcome ways. For others, it is the ability of the medium to integrate pictures and sounds that makes it most interesting.

At the Media Workshop New York, we offer a *KidPix* workshop to teachers of elementary through high school, including administrators. We believe that because it was designed for use by preschoolers, *KidPix* is an excellent tool to help technophobes overcome their fears. It lets them experience the expressive power of the medium in a short time because creating with this tool is so easy and so much fun and can result in such wonderfully evocative images and stories even from folks who feel artistically challenged and inhibited.

Uses of New Media in the Studio Art Curriculum

One of the important concepts students learn in the course of their aesthetic development is about the constructedness of art, about the careful process of selection and association that makes for evocative, shared meaning.

Younger children focus on representing their life in the art they make. It serves to articulate and share their feelings. They tell their stories in their pictures, and the stories are real. For them, the choice of what to include and what to leave out is related to the reality portrayed, not to ideas about composition. At this early stage, students need to learn how to look closely at the work of others and at their own work, to think about how their interpretation relates to what they find in the image.

The ease with which one can add elements and symbols to a digital image, move them around, create different visual tensions between them, makes it easier for students to learn to focus on the relationship between the elements in a picture as well as on the meaning of the elements themselves. As students come to understand that art does more than display real or imagined stories, that it has a life of its own, they begin to focus on messages rather than solely on literal meaning. Digital tools permit them to make art with art, to grab still and moving images, reproductions or original works, and sounds and words, and to repurpose and recombine them to make their own statements, to express their opinions and take sides on important personal and social issues.

Students of art now have access to powerful digital tools. Here are some examples that are available as of this writing:

- *Photoshop* is a professional image editing tool that allows you to alter and transform every aspect of an image.
- *PowerGoo* is an entertainment product for messing around with snapshots.
- *Morph* is used to create seamless image transformations.
- *Premiere* is for the nonlinear editing of video.
- *Painter* allows you to simulate the use of all kinds of other, corporeal media to paint with.
- *Poser* and *Virtual WalkThrough* let you create three-dimensional models of complex scenes, including objects and people to be explored by walking around and through them—and keeping a record of that movement in the form of a movie.

Some of these tools, such as *Photoshop,* are expensive but very versatile. There is usually a much cheaper but slower or slightly less powerful version available that serves students just as well. *Morph* or *Goo* are cheap because they do only one thing—transform images or combine them or display them.

Using these digital tools, students can combine layers of image elements, not to mention sound and text and animation, in many variations. The medium makes it possible to keep the layers separate while blending them at the same time. Young artists can try a combination, discuss it with peers and teachers, compare it with other versions, and become articulate about their own aesthetic criteria for selecting one version over another. Digital objects are abstract, ephemeral in nature. The digital medium has a tremendous capacity to transform them over and over in ways we could only imagine until now. Anything that can be done can be undone. Anything we have done can be preserved. Anything can be moved and changed without losing the original . . . and with very little effort. There is thus never any reason *not* to explore a different approach, to try it a different way, to add a different effect to see what will happen. This encourages experimentation and exploration. Because there is no penalty for changing one's mind, young artists are free to think deeply about their choices and the resultant meaning of their compositions.

Let us consider some specific ways these tools might be integrated into the middle- or high-school art classroom.

Storyboarding

Graphic tools can be used to help students focus on careful planning of a larger, possibly collaborative work. Even in middle- and high-school classes, it makes sense to use a program like *KidPix* as a storyboarding tool. Students can make a set of representations of anything from movie scenes to a cartoon strip, label elements or caption the images, order and arrange them in a slide-show program, and add visual and auditory transitions at any point. They can create different versions of the same slide show and compare them. They can use this kind of tool to plan a video, for instance. Thinking through the story line, representing the vantage point from which each scene is shot, is very easy with this program. The picture stamps can be used as icons standing for actors and props. They can be resized to indicate the effects of distance in a shot. In this way, a tool for kindergarten kids can be used by high school students to plan a documentary, a dramatic movie, or a music video.

Storytelling

It makes sense to think of graphics programs as tools for multimedia storytelling. Children's hand-drawn pictures derive so much of their meaning from the way they were painted, from the emotion in the brush- or penstroke or the visible track of decisions about when to keep going with a color and when to switch to another one. That kind of immediacy is impossible in the digital medium. Instead, students infuse meaning and feelings through what they do with pictures rather than through how they make them. Students can import their hand-drawn pictures into a presentation program like *Powerpoint* or *HyperStudio,* for instance, and animate those pictures, or consider what words and sounds they want to use to tell the story represented in their picture or to tell a story about it. Students can create a scene, move the objects in it through space, change their color or size, and capture this movement either in a slide show or in a digital movie. They can add audio commentary to tell a complex story. They can also add transitions between pictures and think about what they add to the meaning.

Family Portraits

A program like *PowerGoo* can be used to do interesting work with family photos. Students can scan family photos (or take pictures of their parents and themselves with a digital camera) and construct a composite image. The program allows students to combine features from one image with another with great ease. Family resemblances can be explored this way. This kind of exploration can sharpen students' ability to study portraits, focus them on subtle structural differences in faces and bodies, on differences in posture and expression, and on the way the relationships among elements as well as structural details shape perception.

Animation vs. Cartooning

Digital tools make it easy and interesting to explore the difference between genres of artwork. The same set of images drawn or scanned by students can be turned into a traditional cartoon strip, where all panels are visible, using a tool like *Comic Creator* (or any page-layout program) and into a kind of flip-card animation, where images appear one at a time in a sequence using a tool like *HyperStudio*. Students can then examine the difference between those two formats and discover the ways in which suspense is heightened in the animation while the relationship among the parts—the overall composition—becomes more important in the cartoon. It is also possible to combine the two forms of cartoons. Programs such as Inverse Ink's CD-ROM *Comic Books* present a set of cartoon panels on a page which come to life when you click on them. Each panel is transformed into a movie or an animation, including music and spoken dialogue. The animation takes readers deeper into various aspects of the story, while the interactivity allows them to select the character from whose perspective they want to see the action. The plot, represented in the graphic panels, does not change, in other words, but the commentary provided in text panels that frame the action ("Meanwhile, back in Gotham City, Batman worries . . .") changes depending on the choices made by the readers. The advantage of the medium is that it maintains the strong linear, narrative structure of the cartoon while adding an interactive element and motion. Interactive cartoons are an entirely new art form and one that is particularly interesting to students.

Transformations

The digital medium makes it easy to create collages from "found objects" in digital form, whether scanned in photographs or pictures made by artists. Students can produce a series of studies by taking a digital photo—a still life, for instance—and then applying a variety of filters to all or parts of the image in a program like *Photoshop*. The fact that these transformations are so easy to do makes it possible to spend more time comparing them and thinking about how the transformation affects the meaning of the image. At the Media Workshop New York, we work up to using *Photoshop* by starting with a different kind of transformation. We provide teachers with an interesting evocative image and ask them to change its meaning in a variety of ways—by adding a label, by inserting it in a slide show and surrounding it with a set of other images, by adding music, and so on, without altering anything in the image itself. Only after it has become clear how much the meaning of the image is transformed by its context do we move on to actually altering aspects of the image.

Visual Literacy

The digital medium lends itself to classroom work in visual literacy skills. That is the focus of *VizAbility* by 1995 PWS Publishing Company. It employs the digital medium to make its points in exemplary fashion. Its creators intended it for a general audience rather than specifically as a resource for schools, but it is an excellent tool for teachers and students. *VizAbility* covers six topics: imagining, seeing, drawing, diagramming, environment, and culture. An overview offers several different perspectives on each topic in the form of small black and white photos of experts, from professional designers and scientists to teachers and students, which come to life as we hear the person say something about the topic. These little interviews are not just sound bites—these folks actually get to say something meaningful.

Each section consists of a set of activities designed to enhance and support the topic. There is a short text introduction, the activity itself, and usually a gallery of things others have done in response to the activity. There are also some interesting tools: a notepad prearranged into separate sections to match the sections on the CD, a choice of background music (from pop to classical), and a window of "WarmUps." These warm-ups consist of a saying, vaguely Zen in nature, a combination of phrases, all of which sound thought-provoking even if their actual meaning is a bit elusive. The exercises themselves are intended to jar us loose from our habitual modes of thinking, mostly by giving us a single sentence, such as "imagine an old person as a baby" or "imagine how a slippery yellow candle looks, feels, smells, moves." Sometimes we are encouraged to imagine objects from different positions. Sometimes an audio clip with background music takes us through a set of guided meditations or visual exercises. These warm-ups are fun and they really seem designed to achieve a kind of visual and imaginative limbering up.

The exercises themselves are highly varied: manipulating blocks in space to cast specific shadows, imagining transformations of shapes in space, guided fantasies in which a voice and soothing background music invite us to imagine something, movies of creative teams during brainstorming sessions. There are provocative ideas for design brainstorming sessions, from imagining a way to avoid traffic jams to thinking about how life on earth would change if everybody had the ability to fly. There is a nice interactive storyboarding activity in the Imagining section, which we often use at the Media Workshop New York. One selects a set of four images and attaches a sound effect and a line of text to them to tell a story. The point about how profoundly the meaning of the simple pencil drawings is affected by the sound and the caption is nicely brought home when one compares storyboards from different student pairs.

This CD employs the medium so well because it takes advantage of the multiple media it can use, from drawings to simulations to full-motion video. It also knows when not to use the medium. Sometimes the CD sends us away from the computer and asks us to use pencil and paper to draw something. Sometimes, as in one of the Seeing activities, it takes advantage of the interactive aspect of the medium by providing a series of quick flashes of a shape and asking us to notice how many flashes it takes to capture the image on paper. In another activity we are provided with simple objects, such as a pen, which we can rotate completely around their midpoint, and asked to draw them from a range of perspectives. It would be very difficult to see a real pen in many of these positions long enough to draw. The virtual pen is free from the requirements of gravity and stays put. Another activity is about finding hidden pictures—really details in highly patterned images.

These activities are a lot of fun for children as well as for adults, though the basic tone of the images addresses adults. There are all kinds of interesting visual puzzles and other ways to practice visual logic. The Environment section has us look at different environments, including a classroom, in order to arrange them better for various different purposes. There is a set of video interviews with people who have done a great deal of thinking about the visual aspect of environmental design—in the case of the classroom, a second-grade teacher and former architect. There is a *QuicktimeVR* movie of the space, which provides a useful glimpse into the visual arrangement of this elementary-school classroom (where one wall consists entirely of huge windows with large, beautiful trees right outside). A separate screen shows close-ups of some of the objects in the room and the teacher discusses her use of them. This is a creative teacher. She has really good ideas.

Media Literacy in Studio Art Classes

The media literacy issues raised by this new medium are just beginning to emerge. They have to do with the ability of users of these new technologies to combine works with no original relationship to each other, to take works out of their context and use all or parts of them in new contexts. At this point we have a lot of questions and very few answers. It is important, however, for students to learn to ask those questions and to take part in the process of answering them for themselves and for their society.

The new technologies give studio art classes access to *digitized* art—reproductions of physical art and records of performances; and to *digital* art—art made in and for this new medium and which has no other physical existence. (A printout of a digital painting is a reproduction, not the original, which exists on a screen.)

Currently on the Internet, digitized art usually serves some form of communication about art, whether as part of a gallery exhibit offering an artist's work for sale, or as part of a museum's efforts to advertise its holdings through an on-line exhibition. By contrast, an installation in a museum (or on the Internet) where a visitor steps in front of a computer screen and her face is captured by a little camera and altered or integrated into a particular background through the program would be an example of digital art, as would a graphic image that changes as viewers interact with it by pressing buttons or touching the screen.

A work of digital art is as ephemeral as a performance. It happens only when a computer recreates a precise pattern of pixels— and it looks slightly different on every computer. But digital art is also as durable as stone or brass and as infinitely reproducible as paper and ink. The digital files can exist anywhere, encoded in a variety of digital storage media from magnetic tape to laser disc, transmitted across time and space through a range of telecommunications technologies, from satellites to local telephone lines. Losing one version of a digital art object, perhaps the first one made, in no way implies that a different but identical version is somehow not the original. There can be as many copies of the work as there are people who want it.

What does this mean about the value of digital art? What makes it precious if everybody can have an original? Who owns art made possible by access to malleable reproductions, composed of found digital objects, transformations, and interactions between artist and audience? Copyright is not a serious consideration for most educators unless they or their students are planning to sell any of their digital work. Nevertheless, it is important for students to know how to credit sources appropriately. There are no ready conventions. The arts education community needs a new language for describing the medium in which a digital work is done and the materials on which it is based. This new language needs terms that define the relationships among new digital creations and any artworks used in their making. When does it make sense to stop crediting an image? How many ways must it have been transformed until it is no longer associated with the artist who made it? How recognizable does the original have to be? Now that artists can use work done in this medium by students as easily as students can use the work made by artists, these ownership issues are made more concrete to students. Thoughtful conversation about them thus becomes an integral part of studio arts.

◆ New Media and Art History

What the New Media Contribute

The arts education standards stress the importance of helping students understand the relationship between art and culture, between the particular contributions made by diverse cultural groups and the effect of cultural traditions and values on the life of art. The New York City standards stress the importance of teaching students how art gives voice to communities, preserves a community's collective memory, and allows students to transmit their cultural inheritance. The new media provide an enormous wealth of resources designed to let students explore everything from cave paintings to "bleeding-edge" (both "cutting" and "leading") avant garde art, from street graffiti to priceless objects locked away in vaults. Increasingly, the primary value for access to these art treasures is the Internet.

The Internet is sometimes talked about as a new frontier. It is a vast virtual space where each new arrival can homestead. An initial homesite can grow into as rich and complex an operation as time, money, and technology permit. Bandwidth, the real estate of this new frontier, seems unlimited. The problem is that there are few maps, no visible boundaries, and no clear, shared sense of the rights and responsibilities in this new space. Communities are springing up, and people are trying to invent a viable economic base, a set of laws, an etiquette, some kind of order. These will help tame the chaos and make the journey easier for those who are not inclined to pioneering but who want a chance to travel through this space and take advantage of some of its rich offerings. For the K to 12 arts curriculum, this new frontier promises a kind of access to some of the world's art treasures and a new medium in which to express students' own artistic vision.

Artists have taken to the Internet like ducks to water. Perhaps this is a natural development since the Internet is, after all, just another medium for artists. For art educators, the most immediate promise of the Internet is that it grants access to some of the world's art treasures on a scale never before possible. It should not go without saying, however, that a visit to a virtual museum is not the same as a visit to a real museum. No digital reproduction can inspire the quality of awe we sometimes feel standing in front of a wonderful painting. The quality of the material brings home that somebody, perhaps in a very different time and place, actually made this thing, made it for us, took such amazing pains to show us something.

Nevertheless, there are priceless resources for arts educators on the Internet. Museums have sites with educational materials on them. There are on-line courses and conversations about art and about the teaching of art. And there are galleries exhibiting everything from polished, commercial art to experimental fine arts, from children's exhibits to professional marketing sites.

The Internet gives us a glimpse into the economic lives of artists and the art business. Looking up artists, seeing how they present themselves and their work, listening in on and participating in their conversations in forums and chat rooms, provide invaluable ways for students to learn about art as a career and a way of life. It also presents a community of artists whom young artists might join and from whom they can get advice, mentoring, and support. As with all potential resources, of course, somebody has to prepare the ground or lead the way. There are not nearly enough educational arts projects, but there will be more. Educational uses of this medium center around its power to represent, create, and communicate.

Uses of the New Media in the Art History Curriculum

The power of digital technologies to send representations of objects across time and space turns an ordinary computer into a cornucopia. Images flood into the classroom or the school library. There are incredibly interesting things to look at, consider, dismiss, or keep. In a classroom setting, however, students are usually looking for something specific to answer a question, illustrate an idea, or demonstrate a concept.

Finding specific or relevant images on the Internet is not a trivial matter, even though there are many thousands of them out there. Some of the more sophisticated search engines for images present a good opportunity to learn about categories used to describe art. There are three ways to find things on the Web:

◆ going directly to a known (or bookmarked) URL;
◆ browsing through a set of categories provided by a search engine;
◆ doing a free keyword search.

The first is the most efficient, of course, since it means someone else has seen the site and found it to be worthwhile. This digital equivalent of spreading useful information by word of mouth is well established on the Internet. The category system created by the search engines includes many excellent sites, all investigated and deemed appropriate to the topic by the search engine companies. Finding things this way precludes coming across very strange or possibly pornographic sites by accident. The keyword search, on the other hand, can produce an amazing array of apparently unrelated addresses, some of very dubious value, some downright offensive. As a guideline for art educators, category searches are not only less dangerous but also more efficient.

Let us consider just a few of the many art-related digital resources and imagine how they might be used in a middle- or high-school classroom.

Virtual Museums

There are quite a few virtual museums on the Internet, and real museums are developing an increasing on-line presence. Initially, museums tended to use their Web sites to provide information about their programs and exhibits. More and more, however, the major museums are also including an educational section featuring a variety of on-line activities, exhibits, and resources designed to interest viewers in the art (or science or history) the museums preserve and display. The easiest way to find these digital resources is to go through one of the big search engines with category search capacity, such as Yahoo (www.yahoo.com). In Yahoo's Arts and Humanities category, there are listings of museums, galleries, and art centers.

Most world-class museums have some images on-line but may provide little information to place them into a historical or aesthetic context. A few to visit to get a feel for the best in content and features of museum sites are:

- The Metropolitan Museum of Art, New York (www.met museum.org)
- The Jewish Museum, New York (www.jewishmuseum.org)
- The Vatican Museum, Rome (www.christusrev.org/www1/ vaticano/omusei.html)
- The Uffizi Gallery, Florence (www.uffizi.firenze.it/welcomeE. html)
- The Centre Georges Pompidou, Paris (www.cnac-gp.fr/ musee/)
- The Louvre, Paris (mistral.culture.fr/louvre/)

Of all the museums that can be visited on-line, the Jewish Museum does the best job of placing images in context. Each picture, whether photograph, sculpture, or painting, is literally surrounded by four text sections: art history, social/cultural context,

history of this object, and insider's comment. It might be an interesting assignment to take this format and ask students to create
their own collaborative on-line museum. A template that consists
of four text fields and a place for a thumbnail version of the image
in the center, which can be enlarged by clicking in it, is easy
enough to create in any number of authoring tools, including
HyperStudio. Students can then go off and find a digital picture
they are interested in or one that conforms to a set of criteria
articulated by the teacher (based on a theme or an aesthetic concept, for example) and import it into the template. Next, they can
go on-line or to the library and do the research necessary to provide the kind of background information modeled in the Jewish
Museum site.

This kind of collaborative project can be more than a conventional art history research report in multimedia form. The digital
medium itself makes it possible to add to the collection over the
years and to create a set of internal links among related paintings
based on themes or aesthetic elements. The insider comment section could also be enlarged to permit commentary about each
image from other students, either those who have seen the real
work of art in their travels or who have a particular opinion about
its meaning or additional information about its place in history.

Search Criteria

Web commerce has given rise to an interesting set of search criteria for art. At the Web site of an international marketing service
(*Artists OnLine,* www.onlineart.com/), for instance, you can buy
art by bidding in an ongoing silent auction. You can search by
type of art, from assemblage to wood cut; by *style,* from abstract to
visionary; and by *media,* from gold to wool. You can also search
by *primary* or *secondary color* (forty-three choices, from aqua to
yellow); *mood* (sixty-three types, from apocalyptic to wistful); and
subject matter (one hundred one topics, from abstract to zodiac).
These lists of attributes are useful for indexing and they provide a
useful vocabulary for talking about pictures. It might be an interesting activity to use them as a classification scheme, asking students to classify an array of images from a CD-ROM such as the

Metropolitan Museum's *Look What I See* or any other picture resource.

Electronic Artbooks

CD-ROMs are available that present the work of a variety of individual artists. They are well suited as starting points for student research about an artist since they tend to provide a good deal of context as well as a selection of the artist's most important works. At a different level, these disks also serve as examples of how to craft a multimedia presentation about an artist. Here are some examples:

◆ *Paul Cézanne: Portrait of My World* (Corbis Publishing © 1996) allows us to explore an artist's world as well as his paintings. It tries to simulate a world by mixing audio and movies, slide shows and pictures, into a kind of performance piece. The basic metaphor of the disk is a set of walks or explorations with Cézanne through his world. The screens look like pencil drawings of a studio, a café, a railroad station, peopled with photographs of contemporaries and including significant objects that can be clicked on to take a closer look. We can walk through this sketch of a world, and encounter many voices, including that of Cézanne himself. The interface design is interesting. The sketchiness and deliberate lack of realism in the visual image is in contrast to the apparent realism of the audio track, including footsteps and other sound effects, snatches of overheard conversation, and the steady commentary by the artist himself. There is a mention of the actor portraying Cézanne in the credit screens, but there is no disclaimer explaining whether Cézanne actually ever said anything like the words attributed to him here.

The paintings of the areas in France Cézanne worked in can be compared to photographs and to each other. The reproductions are beautiful, the color is great, and the zoom is excellent, showing every part of the picture in context. The accompanying text for each work describes the composition and discusses the technique Cézanne used in the painting.

The entire design underscores the nonlinear nature of the way the information is organized on this disk. There are three separate but related menus, all of which take us to the same information, but the paths are organized to reflect different perspectives on the content. There is an array of five categories of places: station, landscapes, studio, museum, and cafés. Each place contains three different areas, identified by a particular painting. Each type of place is associated with a set of narratives in the form of slide shows with audio. And there is plenty of background information about each type of place. Circles are a graphic theme in this design, suggesting nonlinearity in another way. Circles surround categories of places, indicate links to narratives, and frame close-ups of many of the paintings. The narratives are very artfully composed, including interesting text design.

The design of this disk is not transparent but, rather, self-conscious. This consciousness is interesting, however, and does not get in the way. It fits with the thinking about art contained in the narratives and commentaries. This is, indeed, an exploration, a meandering path through paintings and ideas and landscapes.

♦ *Leonardo the Inventor* (InterActive Electronic Publishing, 1994) is an example of an "edutainment" product for young people—and not to be confused with another CD-ROM about Leonardo, discussed below. Though its content is not very deep, it makes a fine resource for an elementary- or middle-school library. Its focus is on the genius of Leonardo's inventions and how they foreshadow current technology. It is fun to browse through. There are some nice animations, some cool 3D images, and an informative short biography, as well as a useful bibliography. Three games are the only activities on the disk. The inventions use animation and movies nicely as illustrations and some allow a bit of interaction. We can click and watch a virtual musical instrument produce a note, for instance, but we can't simulate playing the instrument by varying the pace of the notes.

◆ *Leonardo da Vinci* (Corbis Publishing, 1995) is for adults. It is marketed as revealing "the Mysterious Writings of the Original Renaissance Man." This CD-ROM is presented as the fruit of a marriage of two geniuses: Leonardo (represented by Professor Martin Kemp of Oxford University) and multimedia technology (represented by Bill Gates, the chairman of Microsoft and Corbis). The focus of this disk, which is primarily for scholars, is the Codex Leicester, which is owned by Gates. Each page is there, available in close-up. The disk is well designed and easy to use. There are good audio slide shows about the Renaissance, which make a fine resource for a middle- and high-school classroom or library. Navigation is easy. In the upper right-hand corner of every screen there is a small map of the galleries, exhibits, and tours that make up this disk. Running the cursor over any part of it produces the section's title. Clicking in it takes us to the section. This ease of navigation encourages nonlinear exploration. But the best part is the virtual lens we can pass over the text, turning it into non-mirror writing that looks just like the "original" or into comfortably readable English, while maintaining the feel of the original by keeping it in view. The translator lens shows about eight lines all the way across the visible part of the page, enough to get the flow of a paragraph. It works beautifully and feels like magic. This kind of temporary transformation, under total user control, is a wonderful use of the medium.

Multicultural Focus

Truths & Fictions: A Journey From Documentary to Digital Photography (© 1995 the Voyager Company) is a CD-ROM that explores the issue of transformation using digitally altered photographic images. It is a personal statement by the Mexican photographer Pedro Meyer about the revolution in his thinking about photography caused by the advent of the digital media. The disk consists of two major parts: a gallery of photographs, including the different images the photographer combined into the final form; and a very nice audio discussion, in Meyer's own somewhat avuncular voice, with his pleasant Mexican lilt, about what he was thinking or trying to do when he composed these images. The second part is a resource, the record of a long conversation, in a range of media, with other photographers about the project of this disk. There are letters, photographs, and audio clips from photographers of many countries discussing the meaning of this new media for their art form.

At the Media Workshop New York we have often used this disk as a way to discuss issues of media literacy, particularly the issue of visual truth or of images as evidence. We start out with a simple exercise. There are ten black and white photos among the works featured in the disk. We print them by taking a shot of the entire screen when one of the images is visible (the CD does not permit direct printing of the images) and tell participants that all but one of these images has been electronically altered. Their task is to identify the one unaltered image. The unaltered image is of a huge chair, a monument somewhere. Every now and then a participant knows about this monument and thus realizes the image is unaltered. Most of the time, however, at least one workshop participant guesses each of the images, bringing home that point that there is no way to tell.

Next, we ask each participant to take two or three of the photos that are particularly interesting to them and answer three questions: 1) What do you think Meyer was trying to show in this picture? 2) What parts of the image do you think were altered? 3) What effect did the alteration have on the picture's meaning? When participants have thought about the pictures in some depth, we invite them to listen to Meyer's own description of what he was trying to achieve, what he altered, and why the alteration made sense to him. The more thoughtful participants are about trying to imagine how the photo was composed and why, the more they get out of Meyer's own words. His perspective is on the meaning of the image rather than on technique.

The emphasis on meaning and on cultural perspectives makes this CD a valuable resource for the history or social studies curriculum as well as for arts education. All text and voice is available in Spanish and English. This activity often results in very interesting and wide-ranging discussions from multiculturalism to questioning the validity of the artist's own interpretation of the work.

Art Manifestos

New media artists are trying to explore the digital medium itself, to focus on what makes it special and what new forms of artistic expression it makes possible. For some, it is the digital nature of the medium they wish to explore. These are the artists whose work uses the transformational power of the medium to make us see familiar things in new ways through image collages or video and multimedia compositions. Such artists often attach manifestos explaining their beliefs about the revolutionary change brought to the world of art by these new media. One such movement, massurealism, for instance, is described as "a coalescence of pop art and surrealism. Combining attributes of both art forms, massurealism has given artists a forum for their surrealistic imagery which is conceived with the use of popular icons and influenced by mass-media and technology." This idea is further explained and illustrated in the August 1997 issue of *NewArt Observations* (www.eci.com/new-art/). The explanation is sensible, defines both pop art and surrealism, and is entirely appropriate for high school students.

Interactive Installations

There are artists for whom the interactive nature of the digital medium seems most promising. In a Jenny Holzer piece, called *please change beliefs* (www.adaweb.com), for instance, we are presented with her familiar, moving words made of light dots. Holzer makes visual art with words. Her electronic word sculptures have appeared in major museums. In *please change beliefs,* clicking on a word in the current phrase takes us to a whole screen full of phrases. Clicking on any of them produces others. If you do nothing, they change too. In the end, we are invited to edit any phrase or add our own. The edit screen asks us to select a truism from a long, scrolling list, or to improve or replace the truism. We are assured that ours will be added to a new master list. Students can make similar installations.

Art Chats

Through the Internet, young artists can not only learn about how artists make a living, they can join the community of artists on many levels, from participating in on-line forums and message boards to e-mailing artists to talk about their work or inviting them to critique student work. These mentoring relationships require careful nurturing, of course. Not all artists are generous in their response to students, nor are all artists articulate about their art. Many of the artists in residence who have been working in schools during the last couple of decades can use the Internet to plan school projects with teachers and students, to communicate about them, to advertise and document them. There are message boards on which art teachers discuss the art of teaching art or offer themselves as collaborators in cross-school art projects.

Net Art

There are new artists, particularly the new "hacker artists," who work as programmers or electronic artists and who love playing around with new ways to use computational technology. Many of them invent the kinds of tools and utilities, or new ways of using established tools, that other artists use in their work. For others, it is the live, communicative nature of the medium that stimulates them most. For these artists, the improvisational nature of the collaboration among them, captured and executed in a variety of media, is heightened by the awareness that others are watching via the Internet, selecting among options presented to them, participating as waves of audiences, entering and leaving the virtual gallery, each seeing a slightly different version depending on the speed of their connection and the resolution of their monitor.

As an example, in *touch*, a work by Park Bench (www.art netweb.com/port/), one artist sculpted another artist who was drawing the first. A camera moved from one artist to another, recording them. These images were projected on four large screens in the physical gallery and electronically overlaid and mixed in real time. Jazz musicians in a studio improvised to the images, and the sound of the pencil drawing and of hands patting the clay were recorded at the same time. The stream of video images and sounds was transmitted live via the Internet. On the computer, audiences saw an interface that provided thumbnails of the four screens. They could select to watch any of the videos while listening to the music. The music streamed in real time, with some breaks due to Internet traffic. The video images came in a steady, rhythmic push, refreshing the screen every second or so, giving an impression of slow movement but leaving each image long enough to examine it in detail.

For some artists, then, the Internet is not only an art medium, a storage medium, and a display medium but also a performance medium. They are playing with its ability to communicate with audiences whose choices affect the very performance they are watching. They are exploring the edges of the digital medium, mixing 3D models, animation, live performance, digital video and sound and text to create new means of expression and new forms of art.

◆ New Media and Art Appreciation

What the New Media Contribute

Museums are digitizing their holdings and exhibiting them on CDs and on the Web. How do digital archives support the standards-based learning goals? The reproductions are arts resources, of course, and help focus attention on some formal aspects of the works they contain, thus supporting the goal of analyzing works of art. The paintings included can serve as a starting point for discussions about responding to works of art. The presentation of the museums themselves, the history of the institutions and their importance or mandates, can serve as a starting point for activities designed to lead to understanding the cultural dimensions and contributions of the art.

In addition, the design of the archives, whether on CD-ROM or, increasingly, on the Internet, can serve as an object of study. They are examples of ways professional designers, museum educators, and curators have chosen to present art to the public using these new media. Students and teachers have to learn to examine these productions critically, to develop a set of criteria by which to evaluate them.

Uses of the New Media in the Art Appreciation Curriculum

The digital medium makes it possible to look at works of art in a new way. Students can literally deconstruct the digital reproduction of a painting, for instance, by taking it apart and rearranging its elements. They can change colors and textures, sizes and formal relationships. For some, this may seem like a form of graffiti, a way to ruin good art by messing around with it. For others, this is a way to try to discover why artists made the decisions that led to the final version of the work. It depends on the degree of faith one has that the artist's version will end up winning the day, that students will come to recognize its merit and value by examining it actively. The following suggestions capitalize on some of the ways this medium can support art appreciation.

Interactive Curricula

There is a variety of interactive curricula or textbooks available in digital form. An example is *Look What I See,* made by Muriel Silberstein-Storfer, who, for twenty-five years, taught children and parents how to paint at the Metropolitan Museum of Art in New York. Most of the CD-ROM contains video clips of her teaching method and of the ways in which children respond to the kinds of evocative questions she asks them. For parents and teachers there is easily printable information on how to set up a studio and how to talk to children about their painting. For the kids, there are plenty of hands-on activities.

The emphasis is on visual literacy, however, not on learning about art. The medium is well used. Kids can find shapes and objects in paintings, can change colors in paintings and compare the changes to the original, see how the mood of a picture changes as the colors change, or as the light changes in a photograph, how the meaning changes as the size of a focal object is increased or decreased. There are color-mixing games and there is one activity in which you can explore how different kinds of music affect the meaning of a picture. Each section also includes an array of two dozen pictures, any two of which can be selected and enlarged for a side-by-side comparison.

Learning to See Creatively (© 1995 DiAMAR Interactive Corporation) and *ArtRageous: The Amazing World of Art* (© 1995 Softkey Multimedia Inc.) are two interactive textbooks for older students or adults. The first is about photography and is intended for an audience trying to learn how to take better photographs. In it, a photographer uses the medium to introduce a lay audience to both the tools of the trade (lenses, f-stops, etc.) and the design concepts (light, composition, shape, etc.) they need in order to assess the quality of their own photographs. It is highly technical in intention, not in language. There are a number of visually interesting examples as part of the lessons included on this disk, but there is little discussion of meaning.

ArtRageous, on the other hand, makes full—some might even argue excessive—use of the medium. This is a rich arts education textbook on a CD. Reproductions of works of art are used as raw material for active exploration. This, even more than in the Metropolitan Museum disk, allows you to do your own electronic altering of images to explore color, composition, light perspective, and the way artists have lived and worked through the ages.

This production used every trick available at the time. It is not a virtual museum, even though there are some virtual galleries. Here the emphasis is on learning about art rather than on the art itself. The reproductions are serviceable but not spectacular. There are some glaring design flaws, such as obnoxious music that is hard to turn off, but this product is worth examining both for how it presents art historical information, and how it provides activities to explore art concepts. Some might take issue with the zany, somewhat silly, slightly stereotyped representation of an art teacher, used to introduce this electronic textbook. *ArtRageous* is targeted to middle-school children. The producers use animation well to illustrate their points. In the discussion of a Degas painting, *Musicians in the Orchestra,* for instance, not only do various elements light up while others darken, sections are added to the painting, created by the producers, and blended into the reproduction of the real work to illustrate how Degas, influenced by the advent of photography, framed his subject in a new way. Most of these slide shows are really very interesting and short enough to appeal to children.

The most interesting part of this disk, however, is the set of activities it contains that use the medium to permit exploration of the works themselves. Sometimes an activity includes a background slide show to provide context, followed by a hands-on activity. Sometimes the activity is a game. There are design flaws everywhere, mostly a sign of shortcuts taken. There is a nice example of a landscape, for instance, illustrating cool and warm colors. Clicking on the cool blue sky turns it into a full sunset-red. The audio commentary asks you to notice how much closer the sky seems when it is red. Annoyingly, it tells you this every time you click again to compare cool and warm, even though it is entirely predictable that you'd be going back and forth repeatedly to appreciate the difference between the two versions. In another activity you are presented with a map containing differently colored pins. Clicking on each pin produces a little exhibit on the meaning of the color in that region. There are five different red pins, for instance, Mexico, Massachusetts, England, Jerusalem, and Russia, each of which exemplifies a very different interpretation of the color. There are other interesting activities, where you can explore the effect of shadows cast on objects from different points or of looking at scenes from different angles and points of view. You can even rearrange, resize or reverse the people and objects in Seurat's *La Grande Jatte* or crop the image differently to see how the composition changes the meaning of the painting.

Design Comparison:

Microsoft's *Art Gallery: The Collection of the National Gallery, London* (© 1993 Microsoft Corp.) and *A Passion for Art: Renoir, Cézanne, Matisse and Dr. Barnes* (© 1995 Corbis Publishing) are two CD-ROMs containing holdings from important museums. Microsoft's *Art Gallery*, which features the collection of the National Gallery, London, was made in 1993 as part of Microsoft's line of "edutainment" products. This is a conversion of the in-house computer information system known as the Micro Gallery, which was installed in a wing of the National Gallery in London in July 1991. It is traditional and comprehensive. The second is about the Barnes

Collection, one man's museum. The CD is on the Corbis label. That means it is owned by Microsoft too. Its focus is on Renoir, Cézanne, Matisse, and Dr. Barnes. The tone of these two programs is very different.

Art Gallery's guided tours are academic and include some interesting uses of the digital medium to explain aesthetic concepts. One interesting feature is the organization of pictures by type. It starts with six types: 1) religious imagery; 2) narrative, allegory, and the nude; 3) portraits; 4) everyday life; 5) views; and 6) still life. The portrait section, for instance, is further divided into a dozen subcategories (state, seated three-quarter length, standing three-quarter length, one-half length, bust length, double, group, self, donor, small-scale, disguises, and pseudo portraits).

A Passion for Art, by contrast, is much more about the context of the works than traditional art history concepts. It has a much less traditionally encyclopedic design and some interesting features, including an attempt to capture the feel of walking through the rooms of the museum to see the relationship between the featured paintings and their surroundings. The paintings themselves are not discussed by a disembodied expert (often the case in such productions), but by two people whose identities are known through the program—Dr. Barnes and one of the editors of the program. These two individuals bring different perspectives and preoccupations to the discussion. A careful comparison might help students focus on the design-thinking that goes into such products rather than merely accept them as neutral vehicles for access to the pictures included.

Virtual Museums for Children:

There is a series of CD-ROMs containing images from major museums, designed for children. *The Louvre Museum: Museums of the World for Kids* (© 1996 The Voyager Company) and *With Open Eyes: Images from the Art Institute of Chicago* (© 1995) are two examples. These programs offer access to some very good and interesting paintings, of course, but they can also serve as design examples for students. The ways in which date, country of origin, and size are indicated, for instance, is worth examining.

These are intended as entertainment programs. They can be

used for art history lessons because they include slide-show features that allow students (or teachers) to make their own tours through a selected set of images, but they also contain a little game for each picture, one of four kinds of puzzles, intended, perhaps, to help younger students focus closely on what they see in the image. It might make sense for older students (junior high and high school) to think about other kinds of information related to these images they might want to produce instead of games, such as riddles or poems or even animations based on the images.

Critical Questions

Digital art archives like the ones referred to above are increasing in number. Students and teachers need a set of criteria to assess them, a way to evaluate these digital exhibitions. The following set of questions can be considered a kind of map of design- and media-literacy issues teachers should be keeping in mind as they evaluate a digital art archive for possible inclusion in their art curricula.

As of this writing, many of these questions are still more appropriate to CD-ROMs than to Web sites because Internet technology is only now catching up to the flexibility of multimedia design available off-line. The fact that Web products are viewed through browsers gives them a kind of common feature set, however, built into the browser, which some CD-ROM products lack. The text of any Web page can be searched, for instance, because browsers have built-in search functions. Giving users control over zooming in on details in an image, on the other hand, is still very complicated for the Internet because images load slowly. In time, these differences may disappear. In the meantime, unless otherwise indicated, the following questions are intended to guide the evaluation of both kinds of digital media.

Context
◆ *Credits:*
  1. Who made this? What is the product's history? Can you tell?
  2. How easy is it to get to the credits? Is there a way to find

out who contributed different parts? Can you tell who wrote the text?

3. Are there any sponsors? Is there information about these sponsors?

◆ *Activities:*

4. Does the program contain activity ideas that are relevant to an arts curriculum for the grade(s) you teach?

5. Is there a list of additional materials for further research?

Content

◆ *Text:*

1. How deep is the information?

2. How useful and appropriate is the information for students?

3. Are diverse perspectives included or is it in the form of an authoritative lecture?

◆ *Image:*

4. How good is the resolution of the images?

5. How good are the colors?

6. How large are the images?

◆ *Audio:*

7. How good is the sound quality of the audio clips?

8. What is the tone? Is it a pedantic, formal lecture or more conversational?

9. How long are the audio clips? How fast or slow is the pace of the speaker?

10. Is there a transcript of the audio?

◆ *Use of Digital Medium:*

11. Does the structure of the program take advantage of the flexibility of the digital medium (i.e., copying, duplicating, resizing, etc.)?

12. Does the program make good use of the ability to transform digital information (i.e., separating background and foreground for analysis purposes, etc.)?

13. Is there a good use of movies or animation?

14. Does the program include tools to permit users to construct their own knowledge or interpretation?

15. Is there redundancy in design, allowing users to create their own paths through the material, their own links between elements, etc.?

Presentation

♦ *Start-up:*

1. Does the main logo screen or home page establish the type of content included and the kind of audience for which it is suitable?

2. Is there an overview or an introduction? If it is automatic, is there a way to stop it or bypass it after you've seen it?

3. How easy is it to figure out what to do to get into the program?

♦ *Organization:*

4. What is the main metaphor of the program (i.e., a journey, a game, a book, a show, a building [like a museum], or a landscape)?

5. How clear is the category system (the main menu options)? How many categories are there? How many subcategories? Do the names of the categories make sense?

6. How useful are the illustrations? Are they well integrated?

7. How good is the graphic design? Is it pleasant to look at? Does it distract from the information? Does the tone of the graphics match the content?

8. How dense is the information layout? Is it cluttered? Can you compare things (see them simultaneously) when you want to?

9. How linear is the organization? A lot of programs are quite linear, providing arrows to move from screen to screen and back to the menu, but with little direct connection between the sections. Does this program provide useful links between different parts of the content?

10. Are there many ways to do the same thing? (Redundancy is good because it allows users to do things in ways that make sense to them rather than forcing them to comply with the program's logic or metaphor.)

♦ *Reproductions:*

11. Can you determine the size of the original work?

12. Can you tell how the original work is placed in the museum?

13. Is there information about the date of the original work?

14. Can you tell who owns the original (if not owned by the museum), or anything about its ownership history?

15. Is there information about the medium or genre of the original?

Interactivity

◆ *Navigation:*
1. Is there an overview or a map of the program?
2. How complex is the menu structure? Do you have to go through many steps to get to the information you want?

If it is a CD-ROM:

3. Does the program keep track of your path through it so that you can retrace your steps? Does the program give some indication of where you have been—or where you have not been?
4. Can you search the text for words or phrases?
5. Is the index meaningful (i.e., not just alphabetical, but with some finding aids like a category system)?

◆ *Customizing (for CD-ROM):*
6. Can you bookmark your place in the program?
7. Can you create your own tour or slide show?
8. Can you annotate the content?

◆ *Zoom:*
9. Are there levels of zoom (i.e., can you get close-ups)? Is there an indicator of the degree of zoom (i.e., how many times the close-up is magnified)?
10. Is there a visible context for close-ups (i.e., seeing the whole image at the same time as the close-up to establish what part of the image is being detailed)?

◆ *Links:*
11. Does the program make reference to relevant Internet sites?
12. If it is a CD-ROM, is there a direct link to a related Web site?
13. Are the links usefully labeled or explained?

◆ *Form and Function:*
14. Do the various structural elements of the program actually contribute to its purpose?
15. Are there graphics that look interactive when they don't actually let you do anything?

Support

♦ *Inclusive Design:*

1. Can you make full use of the program if you are hearing impaired? Can you enlarge images and text sufficiently to see if you are visually impaired?

2. Can you navigate without having to use two hands (i.e., no key-press combinations except as shortcuts)?

3. Are there signs that the producers have tried to be sensitive to cultural and gender differences?

♦ *Features:*

4. Is there a time line that puts the images into a cultural or historical context?

5. Is there a glossary to explain terms?

6. Is there a bibliography?

7. If it is a CD-ROM, can you copy text or images and paste them into other documents or print them? Does source information accompany printouts?

8. If it is a Web site, are links to other sites clearly differentiated from links to other pages in this site?

♦ *Help:*

9. Is the on-line help useful? Is it context-sensitive?

10. If it is a CD-ROM, is there a clear, useful guide that can be printed out or that comes as part of the package?

Using Critical Questions with Students:
Design and Navigation Analysis

The questions above are written with teachers in mind rather than students. Teachers may want to take any subset of them and rephrase them in a way appropriate to their students and use them to guide a discussion of a specific art archive. The following example uses some of the questions to investigate CD-ROMs about major art museums.

Students might examine the first section of the CD-ROM *Le Louvre,* about the palace, and describe its design. Rather than providing them with design concepts to label them, students might come up with their own ways of describing the interface, based on a set of guiding questions such as:

♦ *Credits:*
1. Who made this? What is the product's history? Can you tell?
2. How easy is it to get to the credits? Is there a way to find out who contributed different parts? Can you tell who wrote the text?
3. Are there any sponsors? Is there information about these sponsors?

♦ *Start-up:*
4. Does the main logo screen establish the type of content included and the kind of audience for which it is suitable?
5. How easy is it to figure out what to do to get into the program?

♦ *Organization:*
6. How clear is the category system (the main menu options)? How many categories are there? How many subcategories? Do the names of the categories make sense?
7. How dense is the information layout? Is it cluttered?

The questions about credits are relatively easy to answer. A full description might mention that *Le Louvre* was made in France in 1995 by Montparnasse Multimedia, is distributed by BMG, and was written by two women, Dominique Brisson and Natalie Coural. Understanding that it was made in collaboration with France's Department of Museums and what that means might take more research. Students might note, however, that this disk is as much about the museum itself as it is about the collections in it.

The questions about start-up, about how the program is "packaged" or positioned through its introductory screens, are more provocative. The disk opens with a cover screen showing a section of a painting unlikely to be familiar to most American secondary students. It is a close-up of a naked woman being threatened with a dagger by a semi-clothed man. Another nude woman seems to be lying on a bed, looking on. After the initial credits, the painting fades a bit, forms the background for the main menu of the disk, but without question the naked posterior of the beautiful, victimized woman is the immediate focus of the screen. Students have to ask themselves: Why this picture? Why this detail? What kind of a painting is this? Teachers can try to sidestep this issue, but there is no way to teach European art history without encountering the tradition of the nude in paintings. Part of media literacy is the ability to think clearly and critically about how to handle the issue, how to differentiate between pornography and the nude in art. And if the museum represents its treasures with a nude, why one in which the woman is clearly victimized? Teachers have to provide their students with the critical tools to decide for themselves what they think.

The questions about organization can serve as a way to help students describe features and their functions. The main menu is divided into two main categories, the palace and the collections. The palace section is also subdivided into four parts of the building and leads to descriptions of the history of the section, including the new pyramid, and to the rooms containing paintings (and via them to the paintings themselves). Clicking on the main palace icon takes the viewer to a time line describing the history of the palace from medieval times to the present. Each time section contains several different categories of information, insight (an audio presentation), evolution (a blueprint showing the section's place in the whole), key sites (including photographs of the sites in two sizes), and history (explanatory text). Describing the various elements and options and the navigation scheme, even just about this section rather than about the entire program, might be a good way for students to consider the design in addition to the content.

Media Literacy in Art Appreciation Classes

The very flexibility of a medium that permits such broad and deep exploration also raises some important media literacy questions. Rearranging objects in a painting is fun, for instance, but is it okay? Should we allow ourselves such liberties with paintings? Are there no integrity boundaries to worry about? True, we are only recomposing a reproduction, not a work of art, but what if students decide that their arrangement of Seurat's masterpiece is an improvement over the original? Perhaps it is, provided students can make a cogent argument based on their own interpretation of the work—as long as it is grounded in the work itself rather than in some notion of external reality. In other words, a preference for a particular rearrangement because it reminds us of a favorite time or place is not a legitimate argument, but a new reading of the work, how the rearrangement makes a statement, might be considered legitimate.

Let us close this chapter by giving some thought to the special role arts educators might have in supporting media literacy. Arts teachers are especially qualified to help students think critically about the new media. They may not be technology experts, but they know how to think about the relationship between form and content. Arts educators understand that media have to be explored, systematically as well as with abandon, and that learning how to make good use of a medium requires a critical understanding of the properties and conventions of the medium and of the expectations of the audience. Focus on the medium itself, on learning about the medium while playing with it, on experimenting with it and thinking critically about how the medium itself demands, privileges, prohibits, and limits the "message" communicated in a work of art—all of this is integral to arts education. Arts education provides students with time to reflect deeply about this relationship between form and function. It is the place in the curriculum where focus on the medium of expression and communication itself is not secondary to the content to be transmitted.

More than anyone, therefore, arts educators are prepared to develop critical criteria for the evaluation of work done in the new media. They are the leading critics, the ones who can go beyond the content found on-line or in multimedia productions and look carefully at how the form of these new media influences the content. It is this critical understanding that puts them potentially into a leadership position in relation to their colleagues when it comes to efforts at integrating media literacy along with the new technology entering the classroom.

· 5 ·

Language Arts and the New Media

Introduction

Language arts teachers bring special insight to the enterprise of integrating technology into the curriculum. They are experts in verbal communication. They understand the power of the written word. Language arts and English classes have the distinction of explicitly encouraging students to think critically not only about subject matter but also about the way it is delivered. Literary criticism is the one critical language to which most students are exposed to. English class is where they learn to write, to read, and to investigate the relationship between how a literary work is constructed and what it means to them. This emphasis makes English teachers particularly important in defining how students learn to write with and for the new media, and how they learn to read and interpret the kinds of texts to which they now have access via the new technologies.

Language Arts Standards and the New Media

New standards, whether national or regional, mention the inclusion of media and technology as part of literary education. The New York City Curriculum Frameworks for language arts, for instance, suggest that "the use of media and technology [be] integrated into instruction." The frameworks suggest that by grade seven "students will read, listen, view, and evaluate information from a variety of sources including literature, media, and technology." By grade eight they "will access, interpret, and evaluate print and nonprint sources in a variety of formats." Two years later they are expected to "analyze and critique literature and nonprint materials from multiple perspectives," and by the time they graduate, they are expected to "interpret print and nonprint works critically and aesthetically."

Among the skill categories in this particular curriculum framework, "viewing" has been included with "listening" and "reading," thereby acknowledging that not all texts suitable for language arts curricula come in book form. The example-activities described in the standards document seem to make the assumption, however, that "viewing" is learned automatically while "reading" is being taught. Yet, as the new media enter our classrooms, it is becoming increasingly clear that a critical reading of a multimedia production requires new concepts and that competent multimedia hypertext writing requires a new set of authoring skills.

The advent of digital writing makes it more important to learn how to write clearly and to read discerningly. Students have to learn to "author," in collaboration and individually. They have to learn the rules of good reading and writing in these new genres in which "text" has a new meaning: nonlinear, nonstatic, interactive, illustrated in new ways. It's up to English teachers to help investigate which literary ideas can be applied to these new kinds of multimedia and where new ones have to be invented to help students learn to distinguish between polemic and scholarship, between advertising and poetry.

In this chapter we take a critical look at the kinds of resources brought into the English class by the new media. We will focus on some of these *digitized writings* and on new tools for *digital writing*. Word processing, e-mail, and hypertext are new forms of digital writing. Digitized writings range from literary resources to e-zines and expanded books, from 3D comics to interactive narratives. In each case we will focus on the ways in which the medium itself, the nature of the digital, can be used to its best advantage. It is our hope that pointing to the design features that make good use of the medium provides a basis for teaching students to become competent, literate, and discerning users of these new media both as readers and as writers.

The chapter is divided into two sections. In the first we discuss digitized writings—literary resources that are increasingly available as digitized text. We describe some of the ways new media can present and augment these resources to benefit students and teachers, and we examine some examples of new media genres based on digitized resources. The last section of the chapter focuses on new forms of writing. We examine the potential of updated digital writing tools and close with a discussion of the kinds of new skills required to produce new kinds of digital texts.

◈ Digitized Resources

In her book *Hamlet on the Holodeck* (New York: The Free Press, 1997), Janet H. Murray of MIT talks about the digital medium as having four defining properties:

> Digital environments are procedural, participatory, spatial and encyclopedic. The first two properties make up most of what we mean by the vaguely used word *interactive;* the remaining two properties help to make digital creations seem as explorable and extensive as the actual world, making up much of what we mean when we say that cyberspace is *immersive.*

We discuss the interactive aspect of digital texts, in the sense defined by Murray, later in the chapter. First, however, let us focus on its immersive quality—on the digital medium as spatial and encyclopedic, a vast library, bookstore, café, and meeting room.

What Murray means by *spatial* is the ability the medium grants us to navigate through huge, complex information spaces to find what we seek. The notion of virtual space is a metaphor, a way to conceive of the organization of all this information. Travel through this space takes the form of clicking on links, determining key words, and constructing search phrases. Speed and distance are very relative in this space. Once a connection to some site has been made, travel to it can become instantaneous—a single click. The space itself is vast and constantly changing, however, requiring strategies for effective exploration. There are amazing treasures and there is the ever-present potential of encountering the quicksand of bad taste, misinformation, and inflammatory texts.

What Murray means by *encyclopedic* is the vastness of this information universe, the sheer capaciousness of the medium, the fact that libraries bigger than Alexandria—bigger than the Vatican's, the U.S. Congress's, and any number of universities'—can be carried in our pockets. Now that we know how to send still and moving and even three-dimensional pictures and sounds over the ether, there is no apparent limit to the wealth of information potentially available through this medium.

On-line Books

There are lots of books on-line. The Books Page (www.cs.cmu.edu/ books.html) alone, established in 1993 and frequently updated, has an amazing array. The Classics Archive at MIT (http://classics. mit.edu) has full texts of most of the Greek plays teachers are likely to want, from Aeschylus to Sophocles. The English Server (english-www.hss.cmu.edu/) has been publishing humanities texts on-line since 1990 and offers over eighteen thousand works by now. The site is divided into thirty-six categories, among them arts and architecture, rhetoric, and a women's center.

There are many kinds of digitized texts, from traditional literature to experimental literary journals. The numbers and categories are impressive, but what are the actual advantages of electronic texts? On the most basic level, books on-line simply give students and teachers access to a library. In printed form, these texts are not really preferable to bound books, except that it is easy to print only specific segments. Teachers can easily copy and paste sections or excerpts of text into handouts for students to identify, comment on, or analyze. Students can copy and paste long quotations into their own reports. They can also incorporate sections of texts into multimedia reports. They can take a scene from a play or a poem and analyze it from a variety of perspectives by linking their analysis directly to parts of the text—in other words, they can create hypertext documents.

Standards-based language arts instruction expects a new relationship to these texts, a more authentic way of allowing students to engage with them. The nature of the digital medium itself—the fact that the texts can literally be manipulated (copied, pasted, excerpted, altered, revised, annotated, illustrated)—offers a range of new opportunities for constructive engagement with them. The Internet can help teachers discover and discuss new teaching ideas. There are lots of lessons on the Internet, some good, some bad. The Internet keeps changing, of course, so anything available as of this writing might either be gone or might well have been replaced by something else. Just as an example, however, let us examine one resource available to students and teachers.

Using Digitized Resources in the Literature Curriculum: Is *Huckleberry Finn* Racist?

Kathy Schrock's Guide for Educators is a good place to start looking for educational sites organized by subject matter and grade. Typing those words into any search engine should produce the current address, which may change over time. Ms. Schrock lists a great many interesting sites. Among the teacher resources is a list of sites offering lesson plans. One of these sites, by the San Diego County Office of Education, has a teacher cyberguide, designed to help teachers integrate the Internet into their curriculum. In the high school section in literature, there is a link to a curriculum (www.sdcoe.k12.ca.us/score/huckcen/huckcentg.html) about Mark Twain's *Huckleberry Finn* by Nancy Middlemas for eleventh-grade students. (See the discussion of cyberguides later in this chapter.) It is designed to help acquaint students with the controversies surrounding the teaching and reading of this book.

One of the student activities in this curriculum centers around the question of whether this important American novel is racist. Here is a fine example of using the Web for teaching. Its teacher introduction states:

> Given its controversial nature, should *Huck Finn* continue as required core literature in high school American literature classes? Web sites present two high school newspapers that published pro/con articles on this very question. Students take a clear position on the issue and write a per-

suasive letter to their school board. An electronic text of the novel is available for finding supporting evidence.

There is a page for students that introduces the issue of racism, defines the task (taking a position and writing a persuasive letter to the school board), annotates five relevant Web sites, and states criteria for how the finished product (the persuasive letter) will be graded. The related Web sites include a radio interview with the writer Jane Smiley in which she argues against the book. Students can listen to the interview with the RealAudio player (free from www.RealAudio.com). Then there are links to debates by other students in two different on-line student newspapers, and finally there is the full electronic text of the novel, which students are urged to quote as evidence for their position.

This exercise combines many of the best features of the digital medium. It is multimedia, it structures a kind of conversation between students and experts, and it places the assignment into a real-world context—namely a controversy that actually affects students and about which students write letters or reports that might actually have an impact.

A different approach to including the controversy about *Huckleberry Finn* while teaching it as literature can be found on the site created by the National Council of Teachers of English (www. ncte.org). There, in Chapter Two of a digitized version of a publication by Peter Smagorinsky, *Standards in Practice, Grades 9–12,* is an interesting description of an English teacher coping with this issue. He teaches his students to ask critical questions of texts in a systematic manner and risks letting them discuss how the book makes them feel and what issues it raises for them. Whereas the teacher had once attempted to sidestep the issue and deflect students' emotional responses by calling attention to the literary merit of the book, he now finds that these discussions engage the students on a much deeper level. The description of the kinds of discussions occurring among collaborating groups of students is both practical, in that it offers a concrete image of what this kind of standards-based class looks and sounds like, and theoretical, in that it places the standards themselves into a pedagogical context.

Both these resources are typical of the kind of teaching aids increasingly available along with the texts themselves. The NCTE

Web page is designed to facilitate buying that organization's publications in paper form rather than making them all available on the Web, but it also offers discussion groups and chats for teachers to discuss their efforts to implement this kind of standards-based curriculum.

The particular examples of digitized resources and teaching aids cited here may disappear or move. The frustration many teachers experience trying to find sites recommended by experts and colleagues is made up for, however, by the incredible growth of this medium. There will be many more educational sites, both good and bad, offering many teaching ideas, many texts, and many more conversations about these texts and about the methods used to teach them.

There are many types of digital resources: books, magazines, journals, newspapers, collections of stories and poems, reports, lexica, and diaries. Some require Internet access, and those are discussed later in this chapter. There are others, however, available on CD-ROM or even on floppy disks, that begin to demonstrate how the digital nature of these texts can be used to make them more accessible and to provide opportunities for deep analysis and engagement.

Expanded Books

There exists, increasingly, a new kind of hybrid digital text called an expanded book. An expanded book puts a central work of print, film, or video into a wider context. An expanded book about a film could include the full script of a film, for instance, as well as other resource materials about the film or about the artists involved or about the topic of the work. In the case of a book, the additional material and context might include interactive illustrations and clips of the author introducing the book or scholars responding to it. In this section we discuss just a few, to imagine how these hybrid texts can be used both in the language arts and in interdisciplinary curricula.

The Rebecca Project

The Rebecca Project, a CD-ROM by Lauren Rabinovitz and Greg Easley (© 1995 Rutgers University Press) is an expanded book that deals with film criticism focusing on the movie *Rebecca*. Four feminist essays about the movie form the central argument of this book. Three of them originally appeared in print. These essays have been enhanced by including photographs, video clips including scenes from the film, and other additional materials. There is a section dealing with the issue of authorship in the collaborative medium of film, in which the writer, the producer, and the director of the film are discussed. The section on genre contains a text essay on gothic romance novels and a slide show of various book covers used for published versions of the novel on which the film is based. This collection of covers is fascinating and is perfect material for all kinds of comparisons and analyses. The section on the film's production history is in the form of a diary with video clips. The section on marketing and publicity contains newspaper advertisements for the film's original release, a trailer for the film, press clippings, and publicity stills. The final section of the program contains direct access to the eighty-nine separate clips, mostly from the film, used to illustrate the essays throughout the program (though, unfortunately, the clips are not named when they appear in the essays). Because it was made for college students, the level of scholarship of this particular CD-ROM may be too sophisticated for many high school students, but it can serve as a model for a way to use digital technology to enhance any scholarly work.

What does the digital medium add to the critical analysis of a film? For one thing, it grounds the analysis in the work itself. The ability to illustrate with clips, to point to the object itself, helps focus students on making an argument in their analysis rather than merely a set of assertions. The movie holds still and lets students examine in detail such aspects as how a shot is composed, or how an actor's interpretation comes through in his inflection, or how the elements of a setting support a theme. The background material places the argument made in the essays and the film itself into a richer cultural context. It's easy to see how a similar way of looking would be useful in any creative endeavor, including literature.

The structure of this presentation is typical of collaborative multimedia school projects—a collection of related pieces that do not have to be read in any particular order. There are some links between essays or slide shows, but each contribution is quite self-contained. In real (school) life, even though teachers often plan to have their students discuss and link their various contributions to a topic or theme, there rarely ends up being enough time to do that last part of the process. The research and production stages of the multimedia report pieces take longer than expected or fill all the available time. The gluing together of the pieces happens at the very end, when there is no time left to discuss possible connections and certainly no time to add and do justice to any new ones. In the long run, however, the conversations about how the students' contributions relate to one another would probably prove worth the extra time spent turning them into digital links. This process of associating ideas is particularly instructive if students are asked to name and annotate their links, thereby defining and articulating the connections they are making—in other words, documenting what they are thinking, what they know, and what they do and don't understand about the work, topic, or theme.

The Salt of the Earth

The Voyager CD-ROM *The Salt of the Earth: A Film of Politics and Passion* (© 1994 The Voyager Company) is yet another variation of the multimedia-enhanced text, in this case more film history than criticism. The digital medium only recently learned how to display full-motion video. *The Salt of the Earth* CD-ROM was an early attempt to mine the potential of digital video. Far superior quality is possible now, and as the storage capacity of the disks improves, there will be more film CD-ROMs. In this case, the film that is the focus of the program is in black and white, which looks better in a poor reproduction than color does. It is best seen in a very small 3-by-4-inch window. The program allows you to double the size and center it on the screen, but it is a poor attempt to simulate full video. The resolution of the image in a large window is so poor that it becomes blocky and jagged, spoiling the aesthetic and making the film seem crude rather than stark. It would make no sense to expect students to appreciate this film if they saw only the tiny version available on this CD-ROM, even though the entire film is included. It should be viewed as a film or at least as a full-size videotape. Despite the technical limitations, however, this CD-ROM program makes it possible to study the film in far greater depth than a videotape and the shooting script alone would permit.

The script is available in four different languages (though the audio remains English—no dubs). Every word of the script can be searched. Clicking on a word produces a list of every other occurrence, including the context sentence in which the word appears. Clicking on the list produces the section of the movie and the script. One might conduct a search on the word "sister," for instance, or for a particular character, a setting, or an expression.

The additional material that makes this CD-ROM an excellent vehicle for interdisciplinary or cross-curricular study places the film in three distinct but related contexts: Hollywood during the McCarthy era, the strike one which the story is based, and the making of this particular movie. For each part, there are documents, images, and essays. For the strike, for instance, there is a document stating the demands of the strikers, instances of the news coverage of the strike by mainstream papers as well as the union press, information about the aftermath of the strike, and an essay on its importance. For the making of the movie, there is information about the actors, the writer, the composer, the director, and the producers, with their credits, their biographies, photographs, and four essays on the legacy of this film. Regarding Hollywood during that era, there are essays, a time line, excerpts from testimony before McCarthy's committee in the House of Representatives, and the entire film about the Hollywood Ten made in their defense. From a media literacy perspective, this CD-ROM provides a way to study an interesting and controversial aspect of media production. From the perspective of the English/language arts curriculum, it touches on important questions about freedom of expression, bias and propaganda, using words and images together to communicate and persuade, the relationship between history and entertainment, and the relationship between documentary and fiction.

Maus

The artist Art Spiegelman created the extraordinary Maus books and subsequently turned them into a CD-ROM, *The Complete MAUS* (© 1994 The Voyager Company). This is a different example of taking a book and "expanding" it through the digital medium. In this case, Spiegelman himself discusses the media literacy issues raised by this transportation of one medium into another. In his introduction to the CD, we can hear the artist himself talking about why he decided to make the CD-ROM. He admits that his naive initial idea was that this new medium would give him unlimited room to include everything he considered relevant to the topic of his father's account of the Holocaust. He quickly discovered that even this new medium has its storage limitations.

In addition to the graphic novel itself, Spiegelman decided to include three kinds of material: 1) information about his family and the Holocaust, such as maps and other historical documents; 2) the transcription of the interviews he conducted with his father on which the books are based; and 3) drafts and sketches leading up to the finished art on the pages of the books.

The additional material about the Holocaust and about the surviving Spiegelman family in the United States makes this a rich resource for Holocaust studies. It also brings home to students the kind of research artists and writers do to prepare for this kind of book. The transcriptions, available as a separate and easily printable text file, make fascinating reading in their own right, but they also serve to let students examine the kinds of choices writers make when constructing a narrative like this, what they focus on, what they decide to leave out. The sketches and drafts of the art panels can serve the same purpose, illustrating the process of crafting a graphic story. These materials are like footnotes. The hypertext nature of the medium makes it possible to read the pages for the story, without paying any attention to the annotations, and then to examine the additional materials linked to any given panel, to study it more deeply.

Spiegelman himself narrates his introduction, in which he takes us through the step-by-step process of creating a single page, including the problems associated with getting his father to talk about his painful past, keeping him on track, and then defining, researching, and refining the page. He ends up with a section he calls "complaining about the screen" in which he addresses the problem of the difference in aspect ratio between a comic book and a computer screen. He solved the design problem by providing a slider that allows the reader to move from the top two thirds of the page to the bottom two thirds. But it is not possible to see a full page in all its carefully crafted beauty unless you have a large, page-sized monitor. As with *The Salt of the Earth,* the limitations of the medium make it essential that students see the original first.

In some cases, video clips and audio clips accompany a page. One of the most astonishing aspects of the CD-ROM, as opposed to the books, is that it becomes possible to hear the voice of Vladek Spiegelman, the author/artist's father and the protagonist, and to realize how perfectly the essence of this man is captured in the rather frugal use of words possible in a comic book. The audio clips of Vladek are instantly recognizable. We have heard him talk in the book. The actual audio merely confirms what we know from the words on the page.

The layering of information that is made possible by linking audio and video and sketches and drafts to the pages, as well as additional relevant information like maps and photographs and transcriptions, underscores the layered nature of the narrative. This is a story about a man, a family, and a personal view of a huge, overwhelming historical tragedy. The stories intersect and are intertwined in the book, moving back and forth between wartime Germany and postwar Rego Park and present-day New York, between Art's love for and frustration with his father, between tragedy and comedy, between fact and fiction. The images are simple in style but very beautifully drawn and highly detailed. Being able to see the process of refinement, how the artist moved from the spoken word or the historical reality to a particular rendering of a page without ever losing the context of the story, is one of the great benefits of this medium.

Witness to the Future

One of the last CD-ROMs produced by Voyager, *Witness to the Future* (© 1996 The Voyager Company) is an expanded video as well as an expanded book. The video, Branda Miller's documentary *Witness to the Future,* tells the story of the circumstances that led ordinary citizens to become environmental activists. The book is Rachel Carson's *Silent Spring.* The video is about three separate places in which grassroots environmental activism is playing an important role. There are full transcripts of twenty-six interviews with environmental activists and histories of the three sites in the form of essays written by local activists. The full, illustrated text of *Silent Spring* is included, along with an address by Carson to the National Women's Press Club and some testimony she gave before the Senate Subcommittee on the Use of Pesticide. There is also a section containing work done by students during a week-long visual literacy workshop with the producer of the documentary at a media arts center in a school, inspired by the visit of one of the environmental activists interviewed on the video.

The most significant feature of this expanded version of book and video has to do with a direct connection to the Internet. The CD contains hundreds of links to relevant Web sites as well as a direct link to its own Web site, which will provide updated lists of related Web sites as time goes on. This, then, starts to become a living document, exemplifying the power of the digital media products to incorporate change and evolve rather than fade into obsolescence and irrelevance.

This CD was made with teachers in mind. It includes an entire curriculum, consisting of nine lessons divided into three sections: Individuals Can Make a Difference, Collective Action, and Right to Know. There are two different versions of the curriculum, one for classrooms with Internet access and one for classes with CD-ROM only. The Web site itself invites readers to participate in on-line conversations about environmental issues and provides new links to new Web sites dealing with such issues.

This kind of expanded book/video makes excellent use of the digital medium by linking the stories of the book and video to other sources of relevant information. It makes the information current and allows "readers" to add their own voices to the conversation about the issues raised in the book and the documentary. It also serves as a kind of model for a new form of footnoting, where links to source information and other perspectives on a topic are embedded in the text. There is a rich mix of sites included, from corporate information centers to activist groups and government agencies, from chemistry to media literacy.

New Genres

The four CD-ROMs described above are all examples of translations from one medium into another in order to expand the original, to add relevant context to a core taken from a more traditional, linear medium, whether print, film, or video, providing readers with the opportunity to learn more about the original work and to analyze it more easily. New genres of texts are beginning to emerge as well, designed from the beginning to take full advantage of the multimedia nature of the digital medium and of its nonlinearity. Rather than merely adding to a text and making a table of contents "clickable," these new genres focus on the relationships and interactions between the different media and on the readers' ability to make their own pathways through the content provided on the disk.

The Beat Experience

Based on an exhibition at the Whitney Museum of American Art, *The Beat Generation* (© 1996 The Voyager Company) is structured to express the major aesthetic ideas of the Beat poets. It has as its core three books: *On the Road* by Jack Kerouac, *Howl* by Allen Ginsberg, and *Naked Lunch* by William S. Burroughs. The CD-ROM is an interesting example of the use of multimedia. The subject itself—the work of these three writers, and how they were influenced by each other and by the artistic and popular culture of the time (jazz, painting and film, and radio and television)—lends itself beautifully to a multimedia presentation.

It would be a very interesting exercise to have students deconstruct the organization of this CD, its composition and its content, and write about the relationship between form and content in this new medium. Unfortunately, its content, which includes some explicit sexual language and imagery, will cause many teachers to deem this CD-ROM inappropriate for students, even seniors. For our purposes, however, it serves as an instructive example because it uses the multimedia nature of the medium to tie music, text, and spoken word to images. There are clips from radio and television broadcasts to set the stage. There are many movie clips and several full movies, examples of the kinds of films that were both an expression of and an inspiration for Beat poetry. The musical selections included on the disk provide a way to comprehend how the structure of the poetry was influenced by ways of listening cultivated through jazz. It would not be possible to understand Beat poetry nearly as well without the music and the movies. An illustrated book, however well endowed with excellent reproductions, could not capture the essence of those times the way a multimedia production can.

In My Own Voice

In *In My Own Voice* (© 1995 Sunburst Publishing), the multimedia quality is exploited in a similar manner to what happens in *The Beat Experience*—connecting music and images with poetry—but the participatory quality, the ability to manipulate the information, to alter and recompose it rather than merely to wander through it in different ways, is also explored.

This CD-ROM features nine poets from different cultural groups reading twenty-seven of their poems about issues of identity. In addition to the text and the audio, there are notes in the form of speech balloons that appear over the text, pointing out examples of poetic devices. The poets themselves comment on their writing, usually talking about how or why they wrote the particular work. There is a "word generator" that generates a series of up to five words that can serve as a way to start a poem. There are also more than eighty images, paintings, and photographs, chosen for their evocative value, divided into four themes (motion, place, solitude, and relationship) and twenty music clips (actually loops that play for as long as they are needed), from classical to hip-hop. Students can write their own poems, accompany them with images and music, and record their own voice reading their poem. For teachers, there is a resource guide with information about the poets, and guiding questions for small- or large-group discussions. For each poet there is a "spotlight" feature that suggests a concept, from "fame" to "exiles," from "family portraits" to "remembering," as a focus for exploring the poems.

The ability to link poems and images and music and to add one's own voice to the voices of the poets featured here makes good use of the digital medium. A linear video camera would suffice, of course, to shoot a set of reproductions of images and add a student-poet's reading of her/his own work to the accompaniment of music. The digital medium adds the ability to compare the same poem in the context of different images, different musical accompaniments, and even different readings recorded by students. It is this ability to compare different versions easily, without having to spend a lot of time making the alternative versions, that supports a deep exploration of the texts.

Cyberguides

There is another new kind of resource called a cyberguide—a digital lesson that guides students through the analysis of literary texts by linking them directly to relevant Web sites. San Diego's Office of Education (www.sdcoe.k12.ca.us/score/cyberguide.html) has a project, SCORE, that produced a set of these cyberguides as well as templates teachers can use to produce their own. The lesson ideas are linked to the California language arts standards. This is how the Web site describes them:

> Cyberguides are supplementary units of instruction based on core works of literature, designed for students to use the World Wide Web. Most guides are not designed as comprehensive units but as collections of Web-searching activities that lead to a student product. They are designed for the classroom with one computer, connected to the Internet. Each cyberguide contains:
>
> - a student and teacher edition
> - a statement of objectives
> - a task and a process by which it may be completed
> - a rubric for assessing the quality of the product. (www.sdcoe.k12.ca.us/score/cyberguide.html)

The lesson on *Huckleberry Finn* described above is an example of one of the SCORE cyberguides. Teachers are encouraged to try one of the guides and provide feedback to the project about its value.

This new genre of lessons should be differentiated from more traditional lessons available in digital format. Let us compare two cyberguides about *Hamlet*. The first was designed by a California high school English teacher based on the SCORE template and the second was designed by a member of the SCORE project team as an example of standards-based learning activities.

Bell High School Hamlet

This unit, created by a high school English teacher using the SCORE template, is essentially traditional in form but uses the Internet to provide additional resources. The first activity asks students to write an essay explaining why Hamlet does not avenge his father's murder immediately. The Web-based resources provided include a summary of the play and an essay in three parts, written by the teacher, which is to serve as a model for writing this kind of literary composition. The assessment criteria section spells out exactly how the essay should be organized.

Read your composition. Your opinion essay should:

- begin with a strong opening statement which identifies Hamlet as the protagonist of William Shakespeare's drama *Hamlet* and states an opinion as to why Hamlet delays in killing Claudius;
- focus on his reasons for wanting to kill Claudius;
- discuss Hamlet's characteristics citing his qualities and emotional conditions as reasons for his delay;
- end with a strong closing statement;
- follow the standard conventions of English regarding spelling, punctuation, and grammar.

The second activity starts with a statement about how Shakespeare's heroes are exceptional beings whose suffering impacts those around them, an idea students are directed to use as a starting point for a composition showing how Hamlet's attitudes and actions affect minor characters. The process of structuring this essay is detailed in the next section of the Web page. The Web sites listed as additional resources are essays by the teacher and by another authority on Hamlet. The assessment section again lists in detail what the essay should include.

The teacher introduction to these activities mentions that the unit was designed for a twelfth-grade English class and that its purpose is to provide practice in analyzing and writing about a main character and about the impact of a Shakespearean protagonist on the minor characters in a drama.

During this unit, students:

- gain research skills specific to the World Wide Web;
- employ higher-level thinking skills (comprehension, analysis, establishing cause-and-effect relationships, and synthesis of notes);
- gain expertise in writing compositions consistent with the ability to discuss the actions and attitudes of dramatic characters.

The teacher leads the class in understanding the following about Hamlet:

- Hamlet is depressed to the point of considering suicide. (Act 1, scene 2, lines 129–159; Act 3, scene 1, lines 57–91)
- Hamlet is a loving and sincere son and friend. (Son: Act 1, scene 2, line 120; Act 3, scene 4, line 185)

The resources used in this unit are almost entirely produced by the teacher, including a digital dictionary of literary terms. The students are asked to write traditional essays according to a clear, conventional structure. The Web resources are digitized versions of print texts. The Internet is used as a convenient display and storage medium, but the activities themselves could be done just as easily without digital technology. The relationship between the language arts standards and the activities is rather abstract. There is no discernible difference between this unit and the way essays have been assigned in English classes for decades.

SCORE Hamlet

The *SCORE Hamlet* unit is an example of the kind of technology-supported unit intended by the SCORE project's lesson template.

Rather than assuming a correct interpretation of the play, as the Bell High School unit does, this one starts with the statement "Since Shakespeare wrote *Hamlet* over three hundred years ago, directors, actors, scholars, and audiences alike have argued about the play's meaning." It immediately focuses students on the variety of different interpretations. The first activity is based on viewing a film of the play. The task set for students is to analyze a director's choices. The lesson points students to the Hamlet Home Page on the Web, asks them to devise their own questions about the play as they summarize it, and to keep a reading log. It prepares them for viewing by pointing them to a Web resource called General Advice on How to Watch a Shakespearean Film, which lists questions students might ask themselves about choices directors make in creating a film. Students are asked to select one of these questions as a guide for viewing the film. The essay required as the culmination of this activity must include:

- a thesis statement,
- an analysis of the choices the director makes and how they affect his or her interpretation of the play,
- supporting details from the film,
- correct spelling and punctuation,
- well-developed paragraphs.

The subsequent activities in this unit all continue to use the Internet to provide additional materials from diverse sources rather than as a storage medium. One activity points students to a Web site containing a parody of the "to be or not to be" soliloquy written in the voice of Prince Charles. Students are asked to choose the voice of another familiar character, fictional or real, and write another parody of the speech. This is followed by an activity that does not require use of the Internet at all, involving the use of a Venn diagram to compare characters. The next activity introduces students to ongoing Internet-based discussions of the play and prepares them to ask thoughtful questions they might want to ask of other Shakespeare scholars, as well as to post answers to questions by other students.

After that students are asked to take a position on what is billed as a famous debate about whether Hamlet is "crazy or crafty." Students are invited to imagine that Hamlet is put on trial for murder and has pleaded insanity. They can choose to be an attorney for the defense or for the prosecution. Web-based resources are suggested as starting points for their research in preparing their closing arguments, which are presented to the class as a whole.

The final activity uses a Web site at Emory University, including an extensive collection of eighteenth- and nineteenth-century paintings inspired by Shakespeare's plays. The point here—that painters create interpretations of the play by their images, just as directors do—ties this lesson back to the initial activity. Students are asked to write an essay comparing and contrasting two paintings by different artists of the same scene or character from *Hamlet*. Since this is English rather than art class, this comparison is carefully framed with leading questions, including What is the main focus of the painting? Where does your eye go first? How does the painter use space? and so on. Students are also asked to produce a poem or a painting of their own in response to a painting about *Hamlet*.

The difference between these two lesson units, based on the same basic idea, is the use of the new medium to support standards-based language arts education. There is nothing wrong with the unit from Bell High School. Students have been learning to write compositions like that for a long time. The discipline of crafting a carefully grounded argument is worth learning. What the example lesson from the SCORE project team adds to the mix, however, is the freedom to design a more innovative kind of unit without having to devote enormous amounts of time to developing all the additional resources needed. The teacher from Bell High School took the time to write most of the additional materials his students are expected to use. The SCORE unit is based on resources made by other Shakespeare scholars and buffs, and made available to any teacher on the Web.

In the SCORE lessons, students are encouraged to pay attention to a range of different perspectives rather than taught how to argue a single, accepted interpretation of the play. Through the exercise about determining Hamlet's sanity, the play is linked to issues currently in the news about personal responsibility and the insanity defense. Rather than being led to a predetermined understanding ("Hamlet is a loving and sincere son and friend"), students are encouraged to make the play their own by writing a parody or a poem or by creating a painting about it. The discipline of grounding an argument about the play in the work itself is as central to the Hamlet's-sanity exercise as it is to the more conventional essay required of the Bell High School students. Rather than just learning how to structure and support a single perspective, students using the SCORE project will find themselves taking part in a larger community of learners through Web-based conversations in which issues of interpretation are still argued passionately. It is this kind of use of technology, to deepen the resources and widen the perspectives brought to bear on the study of literature, that supports the movement toward genuine standards-based education.

◆ Digital Writing

In addition to the literary treasures available through the new media, there is also a new set of tools to support the act of writing. What is digital writing? It is key to recognize that the computer is not just a fancy typewriter. The important difference has to do with the medium in which the words exist and with the powerful flexibility of digital text. Soon the digital medium will seem as obvious and natural for writing as paper seems now. If paper made it possible to consider keeping all kinds (versions, generations) of writing rather than wiping it off the slate to start afresh, digital writing makes it seem natural to revise and construct alternative versions of all kinds of writing. The digital medium makes it easy to revise. It privileges experimentation with text. Replacing words takes a few clicks. Reorganizing paragraphs takes no more than a gesture to indicate where a piece of text might go.

When writers first started using word processors for all aspects of writing, not merely typing the final version, many found the change from writing on paper to writing on screen disquieting. Writing by hand is a kind of aid to noncritical early drafts, to "pre-writing." The handwritten words are less obtrusive, less deliberate, more tentative. Typed words seemed to have a frightening finality, a formal life. It may also be true that the habits associated with the mechanics of writing seem so much a part of the creative process that they are hard to separate and that any change in those procedures is likely to be viewed with suspicion, as if the ease with which writing can be done on computers is somehow a potential threat to the quality of the product.

For teachers, it used to make sense to have students write drafts by hand, discuss them, rethink them, and rewrite them until they were "good enough" for the laborious task of typing—or "clean" writing. Revision was a form of punishment for not having gotten it right the first time. When the implications of the new medium started to become clear, however—when word processors turned out to be more than electronic typewriters that store texts—the fluidity of the medium started to become obvious, rendering it less formal, less disquieting. Many writers discovered the freedom of digital writing, of putting their thoughts onto the computer in any order, in any tone, knowing that they could not only arrange them in any way they chose later, but that there is no real commitment involved in putting words on the screen because any part of a written text can be altered at any time. In this medium, editing and revising constitute a rewarding process rather than a form of punishment.

Many schools still don't have enough computers, particularly the small, cheaper subnotebook computers used exclusively for writing, so that students are still often writing drafts on paper, revising them on paper (rarely more than once, of course), and then typing them into the computer to get a clean printout. Word-processing software was the first computer application widely used in schools, and many language arts teachers have experimented with using it.

What are some implications for the language arts curriculum associated with the use of digital writing tools? For one thing, the ease with which digital texts can be revised brings home the constructedness of the text, the fact that even a neutral description of an object or an event is a carefully constructed piece of writing, that it has a point of view expressed in the choice of synonyms or in the organization of the sentences and paragraphs. It can become clear to students that the same story or the same description can be told in different ways.

One teacher we worked with at the Media Workshop New York had done an exercise for years with his eighth-graders in which he had them write a story and then divide it into separate chunks, which were then transferred to index cards. He asked them to rearrange the cards and rewrite the story without changing the temporal sequence of the plot but in the new order. The students had to change the structure of the writing, in other words, telling parts of the story in the past tense and other parts in the future tense, so as not to alter the *sequence of events* while altering the *sequence of the text.*

The digital medium adds only one thing to this exercise: it makes sense for students to try more than one alternative order because the revising is so much easier and less punitive if whole paragraphs do not have to be written again but only the tenses have to be altered. It can bring home the distinction between plot sequence and presentation sequence by making it concrete, by allowing students to manipulate the verbs and then look critically at the effect of their revision to see how it impacts the emotional flow of the story. Without the digital medium, students were more likely to commit themselves to a particular reordering and to resist further experimentation. The digital medium made it easier to experiment and to concentrate on analyzing the effect of the reordering rather than on the mechanics of rewriting. The ease brought to the mechanics of writing (two-finger typing may not be a desirable habit, but it will do until speed becomes an imperative) and editing leaves time for thinking about what to write and how to write it.

Collaborative Writing

In addition to making the process of composing or constructing text more transparent, the medium also supports a new kind of collaborative writing. It is now genuinely possible to write together in real time because the words on the screen are as visible to a collaborator sitting next to the typist . . . or looking at a stored screen from anywhere else in the world as to the person whose fingers are on the keyboard. Collaboration can now occur across time and space, without having to be at the same computer at the same time.

There are groupware products that support collaborative writing by keeping all collaborators' contributions distinct but visible to all—until consensus has been reached and the "original" document is altered accordingly. There are easy ways to do that with a simple word processor, where different collaborators can use different fonts, for instance, and produce separate versions of the text for comparison.

What does it mean to collaborate on a research report, for instance? How can collaborating students express their own voices? The research report seems easy: different collaborators make different contributions, research different aspects of the topic, or discuss their findings before they commit themselves to a particular, shared interpretation. If each one owns her/his own contribution, what is the nature of the collaboration? Should they be in agreement about some basic perspective, some set of values expressed in how they approach the relationship between their subtopic and the overall topic? Should they be striving to find a common voice or should they identify their separate voices? Is the final product a collection or a collaboration? The process of having to make it clear to one's peers what one wants to say, what matters about the information, can be very powerful even if the finished product is more of a collection than a fully integrated collaboration. If there are differences in interpretation and disagreements between clearly distinct perspectives, they can be incorporated into the report rather than ignored. There is no reason why alternative views about a topic cannot be included as a kind of footnote or sidebar to the main text without losing the flow of the official contribution.

What does it mean to collaborate on a piece of creative writing? On the one hand, the emphasis can shift from the author to the work. The question "What did the poet mean?" becomes "What does the poem mean?" On the other hand, the ease of collaboration, of trying it this way or that until all collaborators are satisfied, requires a kind of explicit conversation among the authors, a kind of "metacognitive" exploration of the act of writing, of choosing words to express a shared idea. All parties can settle on a particular choice, for instance, but for different reasons, making concrete the idea that the poem "means" in different ways for different readers. Again, the digital medium is not necessary for the act of collaborative writing, but it supports experimenting, rethinking, and revising by making it so much easier, so much less labor-intensive.

In either case, the issue of voice is central. How can the medium support this complex dance between coming to consensus and maintaining and representing one's own voice? In some cases, collaborators might agree to disagree. The medium makes it possible to produce texts that literally split into separate columns at times to indicate divergent views. Imagine asking groups of students to collaborate on crafting some kind of argument, perhaps an interpretation of a work of literature, perhaps a composition on an issue raised in a work of literature. First, they are encouraged to present their thinking in a linear, clearly structured essay representing a consensus of ideas. Each collaborator is asked, however, to keep separate track of places in the text where they either disagree with the majority or where they feel further exploration or argument is needed. A second version of the composition can then be produced, in which these individual perspectives are clearly visible. Students can invent their own way to make these individual voices clear, or they can be offered a common structure, such as the use of tables, columns, and fonts to identify not only divergent ideas but also maintain a visual consistency for individual voices. The essay has to be readable in both forms, of course, but it should become clear that in some instances, collaboration makes for a more thoughtful presentation, for deeper thinking, because arguments have to be thought through to be resolved. In other instances, the different quality of the individual voices will clearly enrich the central argument and will provide a more meaningful context for the editorial decisions made by the group.

E-Mail

The first computer-based writing project for many students is a pen-pal relationship with other students. Many teachers feel that their students' writing skills are best practiced in this kind of real exchange, and schools are increasingly wired and have access to some kind of e-mail. The newer Internet browsers all come with built-in e-mail, which makes it possible to exchange mail between schools, if not between individuals. This lack of privacy, where a message is open to an entire class, makes writing a more public enterprise. It promotes collaborative writing and careful discussion of the content and the form of the message since it represents the thinking of an entire group. Increasingly, however, students are getting access to individual electronic mailboxes, at home and in some schools. This changes the nature of the communication and makes it far less formal. It then becomes e-mail rather than electronic delivery of "snail mail."

Because it is fast and easy and more like conversation than like letter writing, e-mail writing requires a different set of conventions. In a letter correspondence, everything has to be made as clear as possible. If the recipient has a question, clarification will take at least a week, usually longer. With e-mail it is possible to get a response to a question about something in a message within the hour. This makes it possible for students to communicate more fluently and more fluidly, if not more eloquently. Technically, the writing in an e-mail message may be sloppier and more ambiguous, but it permits a genuine ease of communication, especially for students who do not like to write. As they get involved in an e-mail correspondence, however, they might become aware of the possibilities for communication and miscommunication in new ways. If a sentence in a message they receive is not clear, they can shoot back a question. If they gather from a response that they have not made themselves clear in a message, they can shoot off a correction or an addition. Exchanging e-mail can thus become a process of revision. Since the original messages can be logged, students can look at an entire correspondence and identify moments of ambiguity and miscommunication and learn from them.

Making a 'Zine

Another popular form of writing spawned by digital technology is the production of 'zines. These magazines are proliferating at an amazing rate both on the Internet and in paper form. Whether on-line or on paper, 'zines are closely related to young people's ideas about freedom of expression. The culture of 'zines is to a large extent about freedom—freedom from conventions, from the constraints of the publishing world, from marketing and advertising. This can lead to challenges in a school setting, of course, where complete freedom of expression is rarely acceptable. It can also lead to far more attention to detail and an emphasis on students learning to express more fully what they want to say. The fact that 'zines are intended for a real audience and are part of the youth culture motivates students to express themselves more clearly and more carefully. They have to stand behind what they say rather than merely trying to please a teacher.

Desktop publishing makes it possible for anyone with access to a computer to put out a home-made magazine with nice graphics and as much text as needed. This provides a powerful opportunity for students to express themselves in new ways. Young people like reading each other's 'zines, they like contributing to them and working on producing them. Creating a class 'zine or even a project 'zine is one way for students to represent their knowledge about a topic.

E-zines, the electronic version, also combine various media, of course. Any Web site can become a 'zine if it is designed as a magazine. This can include sound and images and even movies. What makes it a 'zine is that it is intended as an ongoing project, as a contribution to an ongoing conversation among peers, in other words, that there will be more than one issue.

Some 'zines are collaborations to which a number of different authors contribute, but many 'zines are very personal. They present one person's views on a variety of issues, which is what makes them different from papers or monographs. Working on a personal 'zine in which a student's perspective on a number of different topics is expressed can facilitate the creation of a kind of portfolio for that student. If the publication includes some kind of autobiographical statement about the author(s) (equivalent to the editor's commentary), a table of contents, and several contributions, it's a 'zine. If the contributions are mere research papers designed to prove that the student has done the work but without giving voice to the student's own opinions about the matter under discussion, it's not a 'zine.

The purpose of 'zines, in other words, is to express what the authors think, not what they know. This difference is important. It allows students who are resistant to schoolwork to express themselves in an alternative format. They still have to write clearly enough to get their point across, but their point is their own, not subject to censure or censorship by those who know more than they do. For teachers of writing, this presents a wonderful opportunity to have students test their writing skills by checking with their peers about whether their opinions have been stated clearly or convincingly enough. It also presents many media literacy opportunities because the combination of images and words (as well as sounds and animation in e-zines) is particularly meaningful when young people are trying to express what they really think. Taking images from other sources and using them in a collage or altering them to comment on them is a favorite 'zine feature. It does, however, require citing the original images correctly and making it clear when the image has been altered.

To become acquainted with the world of commercial 'zines, one should find an alternative bookstore or one that carries a wide selection of alternative publications. To find out about e-zines, all one has to do is get on the Internet and do a search for "'zine" on any search engine. Since these 'zines are often done by amateurs, they come and go. Some good sites to start with, at least as of this writing, are listed at the end of the chapter.

MOOs, MUDs, and LARPs

A MOO (multi-user object oriented), MUD (multi-user dimension), or LARP (live action role play) is a computer program that allows multiple users to connect to a shared set of virtual rooms and interact with one another in real time through a universal set of commands. For the sake of simplicity, we'll use the term MOO to describe this form of digital writing/interaction. Most MOOs are still primarily text, though MOOs with Web interfaces and graphic representations of the rooms, the objects within them, and even the players themselves, are becoming more common. Text-based MOOs are particularly interesting for literature teachers. These programs come from the computer gaming world. They started out as computer versions of Dungeons and Dragons role-playing. Some of their conventions can be understood only in that context, for example, that the folks in charge of maintaining the database that underlies the virtual environment are called wizards. Like all electronic game worlds, this genre is profoundly masculine in flavor, but the process of MOOing itself, a form of collaborative fiction writing or imaginative conversation, is highly appealing to a more feminine sensibility as well.

The language in which you communicate in a MOO is your own. Nothing requires that you say things in an abbreviated or particular way. The command set you use to get around, on the other hand—to interact, to build new rooms, and to create new objects in them—is a subset of English. It is easy to understand, but it does require learning the specific vocabulary the MOO understands. There are commands like go, look, say, whisper, join, emote, think. There are subtle but efficient nuances, like look vs. examine. *Look Guestbook* provides a description of the book, while *Examine Guestbook* also provides any additional information like the owner of the book and some commands to use it. *Say John Hello there!* appears on everybody's screen as "Ann says [to John]: Hello there!" while *Whisper John Hello there!* appears only on John's and your own screen as "Ann whispers: Hello there!" And there is a kind of jargon, like the use of the phrase *Finger John* to get information about the character John, or *Page John,* which appears on John's screen, in another room, as "You sense that Ann is looking for you in the X room." There are special laws of communication, making up for the lack of visual information. Everybody in a room can see what everybody else is thinking, for instance, if they care to share the thought. If you type *Think These people look good,* it appears on everyone else's screen as "Ann .oO (These people look good)."

This special command language is easy enough to learn and fun to use. Everything else is a matter of description, and that's what makes MOOs pertinent in the English classroom. You have to describe yourself and anything you "build." But more important, you have to imagine this text-based world well enough to interact with it. When you enter the Schoolnet MOO, an educational MOO (www.schoolnet.ca), for instance, as a guest, you start out with a screen that says

> The grassy knoll [DT]
> The grassy knoll is located in the center of the downtown area. Fireflies wink on and off as they fly around the knoll. The amphitheater is west. Megabyte Road is both south and east.

You see a welcome sign, a flagpole, a map of downtown.
Gus, Frog, Scruff, and Ginger are here.

The last line refers to the other characters currently in the same virtual space. Experienced game players (mostly boys) immediately know what to do. They try things. They might type *Look map* or *Go West.* Some might start addressing themselves to the other characters. If you don't do much of anything for a while, a tutor addresses you and says

Hello, you appear to be new to SchoolNet MOO. If you need help, you may type:

help me

at any time, and you will be instantly moved to the Help Center, where there are several helpful items.

When you try something the MOO does not understand, like *Kiss Frog,* you get I don't understand that.

There are gods in this universe who watch its inhabitants and who occasionally interfere when things seem to be getting out of hand or when somebody seems lost or in trouble.

In essence, this is interactive fiction. What happens here depends both on the way the world has been constructed, on its current inhabitants, and on what each reader does. Kids who have never really liked to write may get caught up in these stories because they are unfolding and have a quality of magic in that they are real yet imagined, live yet simulated, private yet peopled by an ever-changing cast of characters. You can be anyone you want to be and there is no telling whom you will encounter. Some MOOs are clearly educational in content and their virtual architecture is that of a school. Gilmour Academy, for instance, hosts an educational MOO called GilMOO (www.gilmour.pvt.k12.oh. us), which has been designed to let students from around the world interact with each other. You can go to different virtual classrooms and discuss a common topic or stay for a general chat in the central courtyard. For teachers interested in having their students create their own MOO, there is information here about how to start MOOing, based on a database program, LambdaCore MOO, made by the folks who invented LambdaMOO (www. lambda.moo.mud.org), which can be obtained free as of this writing.

This new medium makes writing a very interesting challenge. It provides a powerful framework, often a strong narrative structure (in game MOOs), within which all power resides in words, in how you use the language. This is like writing, directing, and producing a play all at the same time. You create one of the characters, add to the set, interpret the action, collaborate in inventing the dialogue, and are part of the audience for whom all this is created at the same time. This is also the kind of enterprise high school computer wizards really like to do. This means you may have access to a pool of real talent, genuine interest, and a willingness to devote a lot of extra time to figuring out how to make the technology work—a pool less technologically sophisticated teachers can dip into without meeting too much resistance. For English teachers the game metaphor might prove more interesting than the educational MOOs where topics are discussed and debated and where access to domain experts is increasingly becoming available for students' research projects. There are writing MOOs, called writeries or virtual writer's cafés, devoted to sharing both writings and conversation about writing, and they are of interest too, of course. But it may be the new medium, the interactive story, that ends up being the most powerful incentive for learning how to write in the digital age.

Hypertext

The word "hypertext" refers to a new kind of digital text, one that is not linear in structure. MOOs are a form of hypertext. The virtual space is not linear. You navigate through the story or the information contained in it at your own pace and in your own way. In MOOs, this navigation is accomplished through writing commands. In most other hypertexts, navigation happens through clicking on words, images, or icons. (In MOOs, the interactivity is much more pronounced, though, than in most other interactive games or stories because users can not only find their own paths through the information, they can also add information. The fact that no graphic production is involved makes the environment far more flexible. The magic of words builds the world and the events in it—anyone with words can do it.)

The important new thing about hypertexts is that they are

nonlinear. In many ways, the heart of good writing, whether fact or fiction, has been the ability to organize a wealth of related ideas and pieces of information into a single, linear thread, something with a beginning that sets the stage, with a middle that explores the implications or ramifications of the ideas introduced at the beginning, and with an end that resolves conflicts or contradictions, takes a position, or raises a new question. The reader follows along, is guided through the material along a path devised by the author. Both the scope of the exposition and the sequence in which material is encountered is defined by the author.

When students are learning to produce linear texts, it is this process—deciding how to create a linear organization—teachers frame most carefully. When they learn how to produce hypertexts, students need a framework for a new kind of organization. A conversation among professional literati about what it means to explore this new medium is just beginning to emerge. It is not yet a lot of help to a practicing teacher. Consider this definition of a chunk of text, also referred to as "lexia," a self-contained part of the story that stands in a complex relationship to other chunks, as defined Roland Barthes:

> The lexia will include sometimes a few words, sometimes several sentences; it will be a matter of convenience: it will suffice that the lexia be the best possible space in which we can observe meanings; its dimension, empirically determined, estimated, will depend on the density of connotations, variable according to the moments of the text: all we require is that each lexia should have at most three or four meanings to be enumerated. The text, in its mass, is comparable to a sky, at once flat and smooth, deep, without edges and without landmarks; like the soothsayer drawing on it with the tip of his staff an imaginary rectangle wherein to consult, according to certain principles, the flight of birds, the commentator traces through the text certain zones of reading, in order to observe therein the migration of meanings, the outcropping of codes, the passage of citations.

(Barthes, Roland. S/Z. Paris: Éditions du Seuil, 1970. Translated by Richard Miller. New York: Hill and Wang, 1974, pp. 13–14.)

Does this help you figure out how to teach students to design hypertexts? The idea is that authors of hypertexts connect these lexias (or chunks) in a variety of ways and allow readers to wander through them along paths that guide but do not constrain. This medium privileges the inclusion of multiple perspectives and being explicit about associations and differences among them. It makes the process of "deconstruction" (as opposed to a linear reading) real and concrete. Let us consider some ways in which students might construct hypertext stories, both fiction and non-fiction, using a program like *Hyperstudio* (or any other hypertext authoring program), without needing access to the Internet.

There are no experts yet on how to teach students to write in these new media. We are all only beginning to discover their strengths and limitations. So much information is being developed in cyberspace, however, that it is clear that students have to learn to read and write in this new, digital, nonlinear medium in order to become truly literate. It is up to teachers, particularly language arts and literature teachers, to develop curricula that enable their students to learn these new skills. What follows is an attempt to sketch a few ideas about the kinds of writing activities that might make sense as a way to let students explore new skills.

Analyzing a Poem

Students can type or copy the text of a poem they have studied and create a set of links from specific words or phrases. The links can be of three types: a) personal associations to the word or phrase; b) associations to other uses of the phrase in other works of poetry; and c) interpretations of the word or phrase within the context of the poem, i.e., how it builds meaning in conjunction with other words or phrases. The word or phrase containing a link is typed either in one of three different colors or in one of three different fonts or formats (i.e., bold = personal, italic = other works, underlined = within work). Clicking on a linked word should produce either a different screen with information about the association or, preferably, a pop-up text field in which the association is described and which can be read while the full text of the poem is still visible on the screen. This kind of exercise frees students to think about the poem without having to put their thoughts into the confines of a linear, interpretive essay. It also permits them to look at one another's interpretations and associations and see at a glance which words or phrases were considered essential to the structure (underlined), were considered part of the poet's specific style (italic), or were most personally evocative (bold).

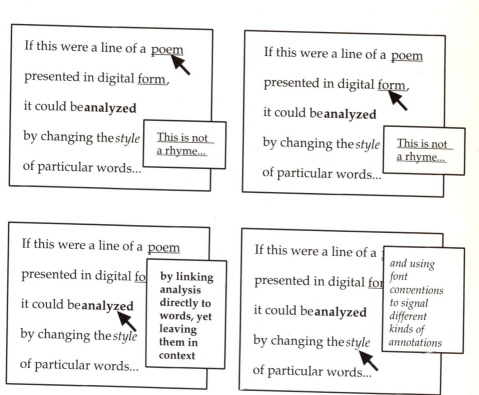

Writing a Hyperstory

Using a simple hypertext authoring tool like *HyperStudio* or *Hyper-Card*, students can collaborate with partners to construct nonlinear stories. A story-starter is assigned. Each of a collaborating group of students decides on a genre and writes a version of the first paragraph or section in which a protagonist is introduced, a setting defined, and a plot is set in motion. Students share these introductory sections and then each student constructs the next section of the story, keeping to their chosen genre but connecting it to the characters and events introduced in at least one other introductory chunk. If one student embarked on an adventure tale, for instance, another on a mystery, and another on a romance, the student who wrote the romance writes a second paragraph in which at least one character from the adventure, let's say, enters the romance. They continue to share chunks and connect their stories to one another.

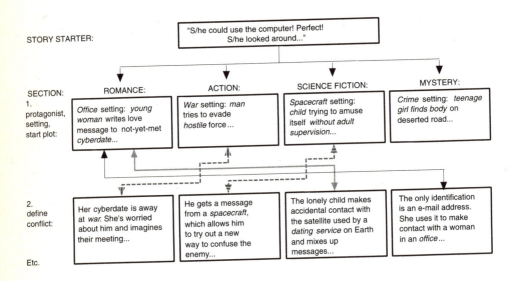

When they have completed a given number of sections (their narrative structure defined by the teacher), they link their stories according to a choose-your-own-ending model. At the bottom of each screen containing a section, they create links to other students' stories containing the character, setting, or event they have incorporated into this part of their own story. The reader can then switch between stories, following a character, or exploring a setting or an event. The story-starter becomes the first screen, containing a link in the form of a next sentence from each contributing student. Whichever path a reader chooses to follow, he or she can either continue along that story or switch back and forth among different but related stories.

This kind of writing is fun, but it also confronts students with the need to consider the structure of the interrelated stories. Some

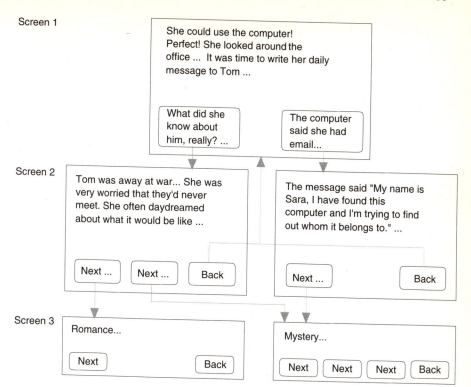

Screen 1

> She could use the computer!
> Perfect! She looked around the
> office ... It was time to write her daily
> message to Tom ...

> What did she
> know about
> him, really? ...

> The computer
> said she had
> email...

Screen 2

> Tom was away at war... She was
> very worried that they'd never
> meet. She often daydreamed
> about what it would be like ...

> Next ... Next ... Back

> The message said "My name is
> Sara, I have found this
> computer and I'm trying to find
> out whom it belongs to." ...

> Next ... Back

Screen 3

> Romance...
> Next Back

> Mystery...
> Next Next Next Back

possible paths will make a lot more sense than others. If the sections of the story have been well defined ahead of time (a clear narrative structure), there will be a climax and a resolution at the same point in the story regardless of the path, but the character development, for instance, will probably make a lot less sense in some readings than in others. Tinkering with the linked story, revising sections so that they contain motivations that work with several alternative paths, can be a very interesting challenge. The better students get at this, the more they become aware of the genre conventions they use in their versions of the story. Such explicit awareness of the conventions of genres is one of the benefits of this kind of exercise.

Hypermedia Authoring

When other media are added to the mix of hypertext, it becomes hypermedia authoring. Any Web site with pictures, moving icons, or movies and sounds is a hypermedia text. In addition to thinking about how to write stand-alone sections, students have to be able to understand how to make appropriate media choices, when to add images and sounds or movies and animation. Let us focus on images because images are increasingly available in digital form. All too often students illustrate their writing with images from other contexts without being fully aware of the nature of their choice. Visual literacy requires the critical analysis of an image as if it were a poem, as if every aspect of it, every object, shadow, line, and color were carefully chosen to add to the meaning, as if the image were a graphic metaphor or simile.

Students often lack the language with which to talk about images. One possible exercise might be to ask students to describe, in words, a specific digital image of their own choosing. The description should include all aspects of the image, including the initial impression it makes and the kinds of detail or aspects revealed on closer inspection. Students might then exchange their descriptions and try to sketch the image described by another student before seeing the actual picture. A comparison of what readers imagined, based on the description, and what they actually saw can be very informative.

Hypermedia production is often a very collaborative enterprise. Many different skills are needed to make such a collaboration work. Producing a multimedia report, whether linear, done with such tools as *KidPix, ClarisWorks,* or *PowerPoint,* or nonlinear, done with *Microworlds, HyperStudio,* or *Director,* can, for analysis' sake, be separated into the four sets of skills discussed below. Unfortunately, few teachers have had the opportunity to produce many hypermedia products themselves. A focus on some of the skills required might be helpful for teachers trying to devise activities that introduce students to these skills and allow them to practice and develop them.

Complex Thinking Skills. Representing one's understanding of the topic under study requires and hones complex thinking skills. A simple regurgitation of information found in an encyclopedia article is easier to do than ever now that encyclopedias are in digital form and information can be literally pasted into a student's digital report. Students have far higher and more genuine standards for evaluating multimedia productions, whether Web sites or CD-ROMs, than they do for the kind of written "memos" they have traditionally been asked to produce for an audience of one—their teacher. As far as some students are concerned, written papers are not much more than proof that the student has fulfilled the assignment. If they are boring, it comes with the territory of school reports.

Multimedia reports have a life of their own, if only because they have the potential to reach a real audience. Students are making informative Web sites about their communities, their science experiments, their poetry or art, all of which are visible to anyone with interest and Internet access. Many students who are less than enthusiastic about books actually like looking at multimedia reports. Students who like to read books also like to read multimedia texts. This presence of a real audience makes it necessary for student authors to do more than indicate that they have fulfilled the required reading assignment. They want to look good. They want to contribute something real and make a difference with their effort. They become much more self-critical because the report is going to be read by an audience, and they become more willing to revise and reconsider because the digital medium itself makes this kind of experimentation fun rather than punitive—up to a point, of course. So they are willing to think more deeply—and to think again, to consider their conclusions or hypotheses, insights or questions in the light of a real conversation among peers. Their understanding of a topic becomes the basis for their contribution to this conversation. Rather than learning enough to fulfill a requirement and pass a test, they can now construct sufficient knowledge to have something interesting to say about it to their peers, a far more authentic motivation for learning.

Media literacy ideas add an important component to this newly motivated enterprise. By focusing on the medium itself, media literacy adds the element of critical inquiry into the sources of information and the need to state one's own point of view to provide a meaningful context for the reader. Emphasis on the multiplicity of perspectives, biases, degrees of reliability of the information available in the digital information jungle, helps students become literate enough to question the nature of their sources, even if those sources are as traditional as an encyclopedia. The conventions of Web sites, for instance, demand that the information gathered from other Web sources be made instantly available to the reader through links, thus allowing readers to make up their own minds about the relevance or reliability of the source. Plagiarism is bad design. Uncritical linking is also considered bad design. Unlike bibliographies, lists of links to related sites, a common feature of many Web sites and one of the conventions of the medium beginning to emerge, are usually annotated, requiring that students make some kind of critical assessment of the Internet site being cited.

Communication and Presentation Skills. Hypermedia reports, even hypertext fiction, require more emphasis on clarity and coherence than linear texts. The reader of a linear text will follow the author's argument with some degree of patience and good faith, as well as the necessary suspension of disbelief. The readers of nonlinear texts do not follow, they lead. The authors have to provide a map of the content, navigation paths, and options allowing readers to explore without getting lost, to make their own associations and understand the logic of the author's links. Each chunk of information, regardless of medium, has to be able to stand on its own, to make some kind of point or present some recognizable aspect of the whole picture being created. Its relationship to the whole must be comprehensible without being so rigidly defined that it makes sense only in conjunction with specific other pieces of information. The more students have thought about the relationship between their various contributions to a collaborative report or the parts of an individual report, the better their chance of coming up with the kind of design, including the main metaphor for the organization of information as well as the chunking of sections and use of multiple media, that actually clarifies the structure of the report and thus supports free exploration on the part of the readers.

To achieve this kind of clarity, students need to practice showing their work and watching others explore it. They have to become formative researchers who pay attention to how audiences interpret their ideas rather than just to whether the information contained in their report is correct and acceptable to the teacher. From a media literacy perspective, this emphasis on communication is a way to integrate a focus on presentation aesthetics into the curriculum. It provides an opportunity to focus on the multiplicity of possible audiences and on how the meaning of the piece is constructed in a conversation between authors and audiences. Because the fact that different readers interpret the text differently is more dramatically apparent in hypertexts, where people literally read the text differently, the author's aesthetic choices become more obviously important. It becomes more apparent that the aesthetic choices about metaphor, navigation, and interactivity, about information organization, chunking and display, about the ways the reader is invited into the material rather than merely about the content of the material itself, achieve successful communication with audiences. The medium thus encourages a positive emphasis on form without becoming rigid about permitting only conventional designs. There are few established models. What constitutes "good taste" in Web design, for instance, is still under debate. Students thus have to be explicit about their aesthetic choices, have to learn to describe them and articulate their reasons, because none of these choices seems "natural" or "obvious" yet at this point in the medium's evolution.

Work Management and Interpersonal Skills. Many hypermedia projects are collaborative. The medium facilitates real collaboration, the kind in which one person's effort depends on another's. Students who engage in rich, long-term, complex collaborative media projects often talk about how, above all else, they value the way the project taught them to collaborate. Real collaboration requires, among other things, knowing how to

1. define the task based on the assignment (figure out what "the client" wants or the audience needs);
2. divide it into meaningful and reasonable sub-tasks (taking available time, talent, and resources into consideration);
3. manage the flow of the work (i.e., the communication among collaborators by planning and facilitating meetings and devising and revising schedules);
4. manage the collaboration (i.e., resolve value conflicts and role confusions among fellow team members); and
5. document the required aspects of the process and product ("position" the product by providing relevant context information).

Individual projects require all these skills as well, except for managing the collaboration itself. The interpersonal skills fostered by the experience of collaborating on something they care about are important for young people. Respect for diversity and for different perspectives is facilitated by the medium. There can be separate authors, each claiming her/his contribution, tied together by links, each an authentic and important part of a conversation about a topic, each responsible for representing their understanding of some aspect of the larger topic. Where the linear structure of printed texts or video privileges a kind of consensus, a single voice, this medium permits a chorus of related voices without stressing the form. Identifying the speaker graphically, for instance, makes it possible for a reader to follow that speaker, to consider what else he or she has said or investigated. Readers can also ignore the identity of the speaker and focus only on the subject matter, on the aspects of the topic of particular interest to them.

There has to be some compromise, some trade-off between the individual, a collection of individual voices talking about a shared topic, and the group, the common metaphor and navigation scheme, which ties the lexia together into a comprehensible whole. This is where the interpersonal skills are fostered, managing disagreements and differences without silencing some members of the group or without homogenizing the tone by reducing it to the least controversial common denominator. Media literacy concepts can help to support learning these interpersonal skills by providing an occasion for reflectiveness. If students are encouraged to ask themselves critical, reflective questions about the meaning of these trade-offs, note the process by which they come to their compromises, analyze their effects, and check their notions by watching others interpret their designs, they learn to become reflective about others' use of the medium too. They come to understand something about the difference between an author's personal beliefs and values and the extent to which they are embedded and embodied in a text. They come to learn that a point of view can be unconscious, a result of unreflected choices, and that it can be disguised by apparent neutrality coupled with a carefully "leading" interface design.

Design and Production Skills. Hypermedia projects require a set of production skills common (or analogous) to other media productions. Students must be able to

1. plan a production schedule;
2. do background research to determine what kind of content resources to include;
3. create, identify, or locate content material;
4. digitize, edit, or reformat content material;
5. storyboard the interface, i.e., metaphor, navigation scheme, and information layout;
6. program the shell, database, or template for the content materials;
7. design the graphic interface;
8. create sections by importing digital material into the shell;
9. create supplementary links between sections;
10. copyedit the material (check for typos and loose ends);
11. beta-test the product (bug-proofing and navigation check);
12. field-test the product by inviting potential readers to provide feedback;
13. revise the design or edit material based on beta and field test; and
14. create help document, user guide, or technical specs to accompany the product.

(Lincar video or audio production does not require programming, linking, and beta-testing, but there is an analogous process for all the other steps.)

Making an interactive multimedia product requires economy and care. There is always more information than there is time to identify, gather, digitize, or edit it. The shell or template is always either too rigid to permit all good ideas or too vague to tie them together. There are constant trade-offs between keeping the thing together at the risk of oversimplifying things or letting it spread out into all sorts of unanticipated directions but making it hard to follow. What is the point of including some really interesting nuggets or ideas if nobody can find them? What is the point of limiting the kind or amount of information artificially when there is plenty of room to include it? In a well-reasoned linear argument, leaving out some pertinent but potentially contradictory information does not become an obvious lack unless what is left out is also common knowledge. In a hypertext the nonlinear structure, particularly if it is hierarchical (as most student reports initially are) makes missing parts glaringly obvious. The reader looks for more than one side to a story. While a single example in a linear argument might seem sufficient to make the point, a single example linked to a category seems meager unless it serves as a definition.

Integrating media literacy concepts into this production process means focusing on the creative solutions students arrive at when juggling all the pressures and requirements of the medium. The pressures have to do with glitz, with expecting a kind of glossy, professional look with lots of little animations, lots of "bells and whistles," which can take the place of real substance. Kids can spend eighty percent of their time working on the "look and feel" of the product rather than on the content, and teachers who have little experience of their own when it comes to media production might just believe that it simply takes that long to do these things rather than realize that they don't have to be done at all, that a clean, clear interface that allows readers to find their way without calling too much attention to itself ("zero interface") is the best kind of design. The media literacy focus, then, on the relationship between form and content, between shape and substance, provides opportunities to let students come up with genuinely creative representations of their knowledge rather than primarily with demonstrating their technical expertise.

Clearly, this discussion of hypermedia production skills is quite abstract and raises more questions about integrating media into standards-based language arts curricula than it answers. The great advantage of the new technologies is that the kind of global collaboration required to invent, refine, and test curriculum ideas for teaching these new digital writing skills can be supported by the very same technology. Teachers can share ideas, discuss their classroom tests of the ideas, and get help from interested experts all through the same medium that necessitates learning new skills in the first place. In the meantime, while we are all trying to develop an understanding of the new features and formats most likely to become tomorrow's hypermedia conventions, it is up to teachers—and to language arts teachers in particular—to prepare their students for a world in which good communication skills include the ability to read and write multimedia hypertexts. Any English teacher willing to develop curriculum ideas that prepare students to become more complex thinkers, to present their ideas and knowledge effectively to real audiences, to manage collaborative tasks and interpersonal relationships, and to design and produce hypermedia texts should be acknowledged as a pioneer of the new media.

Web Sites for Language Arts Teachers

On-line Books
The Books Page
  www.cs.cmu.edu/books.html
Classics Archive at MIT
  classics.mit.edu
The English Server
  english-www.hss.cmu.edu/
Kathy Schrock's Guide for Educators
  (Use these words to search.)
Huck Funn SCORE CyberGuide
  www.sdcoe.k12.ca.us/score/huckcen/huckcentg.html
National Council of Teachers of English
  www.ncte.org

New Genres
San Diego Office of Education SCORE CyberGuides
  www.sdcoe.k12.ca.us/score/cyberguide.html
Bell High School Hamlet unit
  www.bell.k12.ca.us/BellHS/Departments/English/SCORE/hamletmain.html
SCORE Hamlet unit
  www.sdcoe.k12.ca.us/score/hamlet.html

'Zines
w3.nai.net/~alien/ezm/
  This calls itself the home page of the e-zine movement and lists over forty
  e-zines in the category lit-arts alone.

www.meer.net/~johnl/e-zine-list/
  It contains a list of other e-zines.

www.users.wineasy.se/m.i.c/zindexf.html
   Called " 'zine in time," this is a nonprofessional, nonprofit e-zine with links to other 'zines.

www.melty.com/
   Called "Melty," this is a professional-looking personal e-zine by a young woman who addresses issues of interest to girls.

nw3.nai.net/~alien/ezm
   Called "Acid plum," this is a literary 'zine that accepts submissions from anyone interested in writing.

www.exploremaine.com/~aopoetry/fallon/
   A 'zine of student poetry, called "Apples & Oranges, Oranges & Apples."

www.ed.ac.uk/~nine/ntd.html
   This is a British e-zine by students.

MOOs, MUDs, and LARPs
Gilmour Academy MOO
   www.gilmour.pvt.k12.oh.us
LambdaMOO information on starting a MOO
   www.lambda.moo.mud.org

6

Using New Technologies to Develop Science Literacy

Introduction

Why use new technologies in the science classroom? The short answer is the same one offered in other chapters of this book: Because they can help deepen learning and make it more active, more rigorous, more collaborative, and more rewarding for students. As always, it is not technologies themselves that will accomplish all these things but *teachers*—teachers who integrate technology resources thoughtfully into well-designed curriculum activities. Yet how can science teachers put technologies to work for them? What criteria should guide their selection of resources from among the thousands that are available? Which capacities of new media fit with the nature and goals of science learning? This chapter will sketch several key uses of new technologies that can support teachers and students in working toward new science education standards.

A Vision for All, Realized by Few

In classrooms across the country, educators are using new technologies to enhance science instruction for a wide variety of students. Consider the following scenarios:

Middle school students in Springfield, Ohio, use their classroom computer as a laboratory tool to measure and record their body temperature under different conditions of heat and cold, and later compile the data in a spreadsheet to compare how warm- and cold-blooded animals regulate body heat.

As part of a National Students Biodiversity Inventory, students in a St. Petersburg, Florida, middle school count and classify plant and animal species in their own local habitats, pooling their findings with those of other classrooms on-line, and helping scientists acquire a better picture of biodiversity nationwide.

Students in Loma Linda, California, argue against a local development project before the town planning commission, using multimedia presentation software to link each of their conclusions about projected soil erosion and watershed impacts to data analyses and photographic evidence they have gathered.

High school students in Vermont learn to model genetic change and social behavior in ants by running a two-week classroom simulation of Sim Ant, a popular CD-ROM simulation.

Students in middle- and high-school classrooms across the country tap into real-time images from the Mars Pathfinder probe, learning about the solar system, the physics of space travel, and the planet Mars through live television broadcasts, classroom materials, and on-line activities.

The students in these classrooms are engaged in meaningful investigations linked to real-world problems. They develop and test their own ideas about scientific phenomena, and share and debate their findings with others. They work collaboratively, critically evaluate evidence, and propose alternative explanations for data.

Yet these classrooms are the exception. In most American schools, students experience a science curriculum that effectively prevents them from seriously engaging with important ideas and concepts. The typical curriculum is characterized by fragmented topics, lecture-and-lab format, and a goal of acquiring formal principles, rules, and procedures. Media, if they are used at all, are generally used as devices for the delivery of information.

American students, as a result, acquire only a scattered understanding of science concepts and the scientific enterprise, and remain relatively uninterested in science-related careers. This is especially true of young women and young people of color, whose participation in science and math courses declines precipitously during the middle school years, and who are grossly underrepresented in science-related careers. For a democratic society constantly being reshaped by science and technology and facing difficult choices about them, this is a distressing state of affairs.

The Need for Science Literacy

A characteristic feature of the modern world is the powerful and inextricable role that science and technology play in social, economic, and political life. As we mark the passage of the millennium, we look back on a century of scientific and technological developments that have brought humans undreamed of benefits and at the same time have raised desperate ongoing dilemmas. Advances in biology have given us vaccinations against once-fatal diseases, and now also raise the specters of human cloning and runaway viruses. Advances in physics have brought us the wonders of space travel and the threat of nuclear destruction. Chemical advances have yielded remarkable new materials like plastic, silicon, and freon, and powerful new production processes, and yet our increasing use of these now threatens the earth's fragile ecosystem. Digital technologies now enable unparalleled human communication and productivity, and yet these and other technologies are eliminating by the hundreds of thousands jobs Americans have long depended on.

In a world faced with these choices and dilemmas, people need a level of science literacy that American schools have never provided on a mass scale. Science literacy is more than a knowledge of facts and formulas about the natural, physical, and mechanical worlds. Rather, science literacy embraces a mix of content knowledge and "habits of mind" that enables people to understand and practice scientific thinking throughout their lives. According to the American Association for the Advancement of Science:

> In a culture increasingly pervaded by science, mathematics, and technology, science literacy requires understandings and habits of mind that enable citizens to grasp what those enterprises are up to, to make some sense of how the natural and designed worlds work, to think critically and independently, to recognize and weigh alternative explanations of events and design trade-offs, and to deal sensibly with problems that involve evidence, numbers, patterns, logical arguments, and uncertainties.[1]

Effective teaching is at the heart of effective science education. Increasingly, panels of scientists and educators are finding themselves in agreement over the changes in science teaching that are necessary to bring about this heightened level of science literacy. According to the National Science Education Standards, good teachers of science "create environments in which they and their students work together as active learners. They have continually expanded theoretical and practical knowledge about science, learning, and science teaching. They use assessments of students and of their own teaching to plan and conduct their teaching. They build strong, sustained relationships with students that are grounded in their knowledge of students' similarities and differences. And they are active as members of science-learning communities."[2]

At first glance these standards may seem like nothing new. Science education has always been more active and hands-on than most other disciplines. After all, students in the most traditional science classes routinely set up experiments, measure and graph physical processes, and get their hands dirty counting pond animals, dissecting frogs, and testing acids. And science educators have always stressed the process of science investigation—skills of observing, inferring, and experimenting—as well as the content, the facts.

Yet the teaching standards above call for science instruction that goes far beyond hands-on learning or experience with the experimental method. Instead, the new standards call for learning

Science Teaching Standards

Science teaching standards developed by the National Academy of Sciences describe what teachers of science at all grade levels should know and be able to do, and offer a blueprint for the successful science classroom. They are divided into five areas:

1. Developing inquiry-based science programs

"Inquiry into authentic questions generated from student experiences is the central strategy for teaching science. Teachers focus inquiry predominantly on real phenomena, in classrooms, outdoors, or in laboratory settings, where students are given investigations or guided toward fashioning investigations that are demanding but within their capabilities." To do this, teachers need to select science content and adapt and design curricula to meet the interests, knowledge, understanding, abilities, and experiences of students.

2. Guiding and facilitating student learning

Teachers "focus and support inquiries while interacting with students, orchestrate discourse among students about scientific ideas, challenge students to accept and share responsibility for their own learning, and encourage and model the skills of scientific inquiry as well as the curiosity, openness to new ideas and data, and skepticism that characterize science." The orchestration of scientific discourse is a particularly important stage of inquiry. Oral and written discourse focuses the attention of students on how they know what they know and how their knowledge connects to larger ideas, other domains, and the world beyond the classroom. "Teachers can directly support and guide this discourse in two ways: They require students to record their work—teaching the necessary skills as appropriate—and they promote many different forms of communication (for example, spoken, written, pictorial, graphic, mathematical, and electronic)."

3. Assessing teaching and student learning

Assessment of student performance should be ongoing, and embedded in the work itself. This means students need opportunities to express their understanding of science concepts through presentations, demonstrations, and discussions.

4. Developing environments that enable students to learn science

Teachers structure time for extended investigations, enable students to make use of rich materials and resources, and identify and use resources outside the school.

5. Creating communities of science learners

Teachers "nurture collaboration among students; structure and facilitate ongoing formal and informal discussion based on a shared understanding of rules of scientific discourse; enable students to have a significant voice in decisions about the content and context of their work, and require students to take responsibility for the learning of all members of the community; model and emphasize the skills, attitudes, and values of scientific inquiry."[3]

that is "minds-on." They focus on students' practice of scientific inquiry, where reflective and critical thinking is at the fore:

> Inquiry is central to science learning. When engaging in inquiry, students describe objects and events, ask questions, construct explanations, test those explanations against current scientific knowledge, and communicate their ideas to others. They identify their assumptions, use critical and logical thinking, and consider alternative explanations. In this way, students actively develop their understanding of science by combining scientific knowledge with reasoning and thinking skills.[4]

◆ Old Wine in New Bottles?

Before we look at the ways specific kinds of educational media can address these goals for science instruction, it is worthwhile asking whether and how the most ubiquitous science-related media product—the CD-ROM encyclopedia—can play a worthwhile role in science inquiry. There are hundreds of science encyclopedias on the market, covering topics ranging from astronomy to zoology. Some are well designed and contain useful multimedia presentations of carefully selected materials; many, however, are merely compilations of photos or film clips that existed in other media—essentially old wine in new bottles. How can teachers avoid choosing CD-ROM products that are not really valuable? Once a good encyclopedia has been found, how should it be used?

Here is a description, culled from a commercial Web site, of a typical CD-ROM science encyclopedia. Titled *Discover the Joy of Science* and published by Zane Publishing, this CD-ROM focuses on life science and biology topics. Note how the language suggests that the materials are designed to support active learning and coherent connections between subject matter.

> Created by educators and scientists, this stimulating multimedia science collection will spark your curiosity about nature. Whether you're interested in understanding more about the mysteries of photosynthesis and plant anatomy or the classification of living organisms, you'll be able to

probe, at your own pace, these important scientific topics. Through this fact-finding journey you'll discover the hows and whys of plant and animal evolution and the organization of the five kingdoms of life. From the earth's ecosystems to your own body, you'll gain a scientific outlook on life and begin to see the interdependence of all life-forms. Exploring minds will come away with a greater appreciation of the world around them as they unravel nature's many hidden secrets.

Peer through the "lens" of a multimedia microscope to probe these popular biology subjects. Each is presented in an engaging format that enables you to learn at your own pace. The sciences are particularly well suited to interactivity because complex subjects can be studied with greater ease. You can stop a presentation and jump to a previous page, undertake word search, link to a customized glossary for the definitions and meanings of terms, and experiment with quizzes to test your understanding of the material.[5]

Does this CD-ROM really support active learning and connection-making? On careful reading, the passage is fairly honest in describing a rather traditional resource: a database of information that users can browse by category. The CD-ROM offers little more than a printed encyclopedia would offer, except perhaps the large number of images ("2000, many full screen"). The phrases "probe at your own pace," "jump to a previous page," and "link to a customized glossary" are clues that the product offers nothing special. While they sound impressive, these phrases are really names for things that readers do all the time with books. The quizzes that test your understanding of the material *might* be a value-added feature. But they are hardly supports for rich inquiry-based science learning.

This is not to suggest that reference works like CD-ROM encyclopedias have no role in the inquiry-based science classroom. They do have a role, in the ways any good encyclopedia does: as places students can go for succinct and comprehensive explanations of the phenomena they are testing and interpreting as part

of a well-designed classroom activity. In addition, good encyclopedias may offer students some of the powerful features we will
be describing below, such as interactive visualizations that students can manipulate to understand the relationships involved
(e.g., of the solar system). However, the more "encyclopedic" a
CD-ROM is, the less likely it is to have such features, which are
expensive to produce and data-intensive. Teachers need to be
aware that many encyclopedias are inferior to printed encyclopedias in the quality of the content they provide and in the compar-
ative difficulty students have in accessing them. Therefore,
students should always be encouraged to look for background
knowledge in multiple sources.

◆ The Roles New Technologies Can Play

What follows is a discussion of the key goals of science instruction
with examples that illustrate how new media can help achieve
them. It should be understood that the examples offered are not
necessarily the best projects or products available but simply ones
that serve as useful illustrations of some of the main principles we
are considering. A fuller but still quite partial listing of science
resources concludes this chapter.

Goal: Anchoring Science-Learning in Real-World Activities

As a third-grader, one of the authors was a very anxious science
student. I struggled nervously to perform and explain the simple
procedures we were required to do in class, like comparing how
long flames burned when covered with different-sized bell jars.
Science for me was unconnected to anything else in my life, including my interest in monarch butterflies, an interest nurtured
by countless bug-hunting expeditions with my neighborhood
friends. Instead, I feared those science presentations almost as
much as I feared the principal of the school, Mr. Echternaut, a
huge, grim-faced man who rarely spoke to anyone under five feet
tall. One Saturday afternoon my friends and I were shocked to
discover Mr. Echternaut poking about in a milkweed patch near
some abandoned cars, one of our favorite places to catch insects.

It turned out that our principal was an amateur entomologist, and in fact was capturing and tagging monarchs as part of a larger amateur project to study their migration south to Mexico and north into Canada.

Mr. Echternaut had never thought of sharing his interests with students in the school; but soon he was taking handfuls of us for weekend trips to catch and tag and chart the progress of the monarchs. It was a revelation I never forgot, for it allowed me to think about science in whole new way, as something people did—something *I* could do—to answer real questions. The most amazing thing to me was the realization that *no one knew* how far the monarchs flew, or the route they took, or whether the butterflies that returned north every season were the same ones that flew south the season before or their offspring. *No one knew.* That meant my guesses were as good as anyone else's. Science wasn't a closed book, a set of well-understood rules or formulas that I simply had to learn and memorize. It was a way of finding out about the world, my world.

For teachers, the task of making science learning meaningful to students can be a daunting one. Science, after all, is often characterized as a procedure-driven enterprise that takes place mainly in the laboratory, an activity associated with men in white lab coats bending over beakers and instruments. Yet real scientists frequently spend a great deal of time in settings beyond the laboratory—chiefly in the field, but also in creative rumination and in conversation with colleagues. Science in the real world is also imbued with values and choices in ways students seldom suspect. Scientists perceive their work as meaningful often because of the concrete or hoped-for benefits that it may one day yield—preserving biodiversity, lowering the cost of energy, reducing chemical waste, and so on. These are the qualities that have the potential to change students' perception of science as cold and mechanical work performed by cold and mechanical people.

Teachers do have opportunities to take scientific investigation outside the classroom: onto the playground to study the solar system via shadows or teeter-totter physics; to a local pond, field, or stream to study organisms in their local habitats; to neighborhood businesses to assess waste or pollution emissions, for example. Yet these investigations are limited by the local environment, school policies, and the unwieldiness of working with large groups of students out-of-doors.

Technologies can help connect classroom study with the larger world of scientific inquiry, including ongoing work by adult scientists. They can bring images of distant environments—from the other side of the earth, or the other side of the solar system—up close for students to investigate. They can bring data from far-flung science investigations into the classroom in a timely way. They can enable students to contribute their own local data to larger pools of data. And they can support ongoing conversations between students and between students and adults about the meaning of scientific work.

Passport to Knowledge

Passport to Knowledge is an innovative educational program that focuses on middle school science learning by combining video broadcast events with extensive print and on-line resources as well as interactive applications of the Internet. The project is funded by the National Science Foundation (NSF) and the National Aeronautics and Space Administration (NASA). Each year the project offers teachers at least two different multiple-media field trips that range in length from several weeks to some that span the entire school year and beyond. Annually thousands of teachers use at least some of *Passport to Knowledge*'s components. *Passport to Knowledge* is one of a small number of education projects that are structured around engaging working scientists, engineers, and technical support staff with students and teachers who are themselves engaged in related hands-on investigations of scientific topics appropriate to a middle-school science curriculum.

Here is a snapshot of one *Passport to Knowledge* classroom as described by Rhonda Toon, a public-school teacher from Lamar County, Georgia. It was published in *Business Week*:

> At my rural Georgia school, over 60% of the students receive free or reduced-price lunch, and many of them know little of the world beyond our county. Textiles still play a

part in the local economy, but mill closings have devastated many families.

My task as a teacher is enormous. How do I expose these children to the wonders and opportunities available to them? How do I keep bright, talented children focused on education?

One way has been to use technology. For six years, I have had the Internet in my classroom. I have never received any formal computer training. I did what many people do: I purchased a home computer and began to see the classroom applications it could have. But to get the Internet to my classroom, I had to write grant proposals, beg, and borrow.

The program that has brought the most change in my classroom is *Passport to Knowledge* (PTK), sponsored by NASA and the National Science Foundation. Kids get to know working researchers. They read their journals online, have their questions answered, and watch researchers on closed-circuit TV from such places as Antarctica, aboard aircraft flying in the stratosphere, or at the Jet Propulsion Laboratory.

PTK includes hands-on student activities. My students have constructed aircraft to hold eggs and dropped them from cherry-pickers to simulate the work of NASA engineers. They have submersed their hands in icy water to study the effects of the cold at the South Pole. The PTK crew has helped me to become a better teacher. But most important, they have helped me show rural kids in Georgia that they can become scientists.

This past year, as my concern over the need for technology integration has grown, I have gone a step further, leaving the classroom to become regional coordinator of the Gordon Georgia Youth Science & Technology Center. I will train teachers to use technology in their lessons.

This country has plenty of willing and able teachers, but they need resources. I know what it is like to have kids come into my room and not be able to name a single scientist. And I have cried when I have had students—after participation in the PTK projects—list not only the names of the scientists they met through this program but their classmates as well. They now see themselves and each other as scientists.

America needs a scientifically literate populace. The use of technology can help us achieve this goal.[6]

Now, taken by itself it would be easy to dismiss this testimony from a single "teacher convert" as just one more bit of technology boosterism. After all, her description mirrors the kind of mythic image we frequently get of educational innovation through technology: seamless success brought about through the application of the latest technical wizardry. But on closer inspection, what is interesting in this teacher's statement is the way technology stays in the *background* and a wide range of human activities and relationships are in the foreground: new relationships and interactions between students and scientists, between students and materials, between students and new conceptions of science and themselves.

Clearly, technology is serving to *enable* these new kinds of activities and relationships. The people involved in the project—their carefully planned interactions—are the significant factors, not the technology. It is important, therefore, to tease out some of the roles that technology is playing in support of the teachers and students and scientists who are interacting in a *Passport to Knowledge* project. To do this we will look a bit more closely at a recent *Passport to Knowledge* virtual field trip, *Live from Mars.*

The deployment of media tools in *Live from Mars* exhibits important characteristics, described below, that help anchor students' learning in the real world.

Integrated Use of Media. A key feature of *Passport to Knowledge* is the way different media and communication tools are utilized in an integrated fashion so as to take advantage of their different strengths. *Live from Mars* incorporates the use of broadcast television, videotape, on-line resources and tools, and teacher and student print materials. There are five broadcast programs, including two timed to coincide with the Pathfinder space probe's approach to Mars in July 1997. Students hook into the drama of the Mars expedition through the dramatic impact of real-time television broadcasts; videotape overviews of different topics set a more reflective tone; the print teacher guide provides a variety of flexible classroom extensions of the topics introduced in the video as well as maps and wall charts for the classroom; the Web site offers resource materials, collaborative on-line activities, and access to scientists through Web chats and on-line journals; e-mail is used as an additional means of communicating with scientists. In this way each of the unique strengths of the different media is marshaled to a greater end: facilitating collaborative student inquiry.

Thematically Linked Activities. For teachers and students, a major benefit of *Passport to Knowledge* curricula is that the curricula thematically tie together different kinds of science investigations taking place over weeks and months. This enables students—and teachers—to see meaningful connections between science activities and topics that are normally experienced as fragmented and isolated from one another. An eighth-grade teacher from rural Colorado whose class had been part of *Live from Mars* expressed this well:

> [*Live from Mars*] provided me with an integrated curriculum. I thought it was great that through a particular topic, Mars, we were able to cover a variety of scientific topics for this grade level as opposed to just teaching separate, isolated scientific concepts. I think it works better for students to pull it together through a topic like this. So with *Live from Mars* you have some physics, some life science, and some history, technology, robotics. While there are a lot of people who would disagree with me about a push for core knowledge, I think this works better. It helped my students achieve in science through a hands-on approach.[7]

On-line Collaborative Activities. An on-line activity called the Planet Explorer Toolkit, or PET, is designed to simulate the work of spacecraft designers and parallel the planning process through which Mars Pathfinder had been outfitted with certain instruments. Students are told their goal is to document a site conveniently near them, with instruments that had to fit inside a regular shoe box and be less than $200 in total value. (Students are to borrow, not buy the sensors.) Teachers and students, mentored by university and NASA scientists, share ideas, reach decisions on a standard "kit of parts," and then "launch" their instrument package to a site on "a planet near them." Results are posted on-line, together with pictures of the student "mission teams." The four-month-long project climaxes with a set of "mystery sites," which students have to identify by comparing patterns of data with those already logged.

In this type of activity, a Web-based "competition" serves to stimulate significant constructive work on the part of students in their own schools over an extended period of time. The Web environment acts as a "staging ground" in which instructions and guidelines are disseminated, participants can converse about progress, and final outcomes are shared and celebrated. Here are the comments of one teacher whose students worked hard on the PET project, incorporating it into an end-of-the-year "Mission to Mars" night in which her fifth-grade students taught their parents about a variety of science topics they had learned:

To: discuss-lfm@quest.arc.nasa.gov
From: mkennedy@head.globalcom.net (Marilyn Kennedy)
Subject: You were there . . .

You Were There . . . at our "Mission to Mars" Night
This past week students, parents, and guests of three school communities joined together in first ever "Mission to Mars" night. This special event not only celebrated our involvement with PTK "Live from Mars" project, but it also highlighted the efforts of what can happen when three county schools are drawn into collaboration through the tools of technology. . . .
    Tuesday was our culminating Big Night out. . . . The students worked together to set up the centers for the invited parents and guests. Students selected their "favorite" Mars activities to demonstrate, using our PTK teachers' guide, activities suggested by you, and activities I found at NSTA. It was fun watching parents "be students" and students "be teachers" at each activity center. Students instructed their guests on making craters, and helping them discover shield volcanoes and lava layering. The students as teachers modeled the solar system with their solar sys-

tem snack just as we had done with them. They had their parents conduct investigations into the possibilities of "life" on Mars. My own class had spent this last five months creating 3-D futuristic International Space Stations complete with descriptions and explanations with their essays on importance of "Space Exploration" (an idea I borrowed from Chris Rowan). Students explained various Mars Internet sites and helped their guests use pieces of space astronomy software. And the finale of our "Mission to Mars" was the students showing off their "Mars Rover Center" with their town "Sojourner" rover and they instructed their parents on the programming of the rover over their Martian terrain.

What an awesome night! I could not have been more proud of these fourth- and fifth-grade students as they worked together as hosts of this special celebration, enlightening the audience with their knowledge about this year's "Mission to Mars."[8]

What are students learning from these on-line collaborative activities and their associated local inquiries and presentations? It is difficult to know from descriptions like these. But researchers who analyzed the significant amount of student-produced e-mail generated by the PET activity found that the several levels of sequential work, including student problem-solving, analysis, and peer review, provided a great deal of evidence for the types of content and process outcomes that are stressed on the recent National Science Education Standards created by the National Research Council. Using content and performance benchmarks from the Illinois Academic Standards in Science and the Instructional Goals and Objectives for West Virginia Schools (which are local interpretations and applications of the National Science Education Standards), researchers analyzed the content of the students' e-mail communications and postings. Classes that participated in the complete cycle all had messages that showed multiple outcomes in the four main categories of design (D), process (P), interpretation (I), and sharing (S). The specific items that occurred the most often in the written student messages were as follows:

Percent of Student E-mail Items Showing Indicators (from the Illinois Academic Standards in Science)

32%	D-1	Develops questions on scientific topics
48%	D-2	Chooses the steps necessary to answer a question
71%	D-5	Proposes a design to solve a problem based on given criteria
76%	P-1	Demonstrates accurate recording and reporting of observations
76%	P-3	Collects data for investigation using measuring instruments
56%	P-4	Collects data using consistent measuring and recording techniques
36%	I-1	Describes an observed event
54%	I-2	Records and arranges data into logical patterns and describes the patterns
28%	I-3	Compares individual and group observations and results
76%	I-4	Participates in and understands the importance of peer reviews in improving the scientific process
64%	S-1	Describes individual and group investigations clearly and accurately in oral or written reports
36%	S-2	Constructs charts and graphs to display data and uses these to produce reasonable explanations
54%	S-3	Reports the process and results of a scientific investigation in oral and written presentations
62%	S-4	Makes, presents, and defends conclusions drawn from investigation to a classroom audience in written or oral form
34%	ES-3	Analyzes and explains naturally occurring earth and space events
24%	ES-4	Describes and explains interactions of earth components and solar system components
48%	ES-5	Compares and explains short- and long-term planetary and celestial variations (e.g., latitudinal effects on weather and climate, relative positions of the planets and stars)

If students' writing and "talk" about their work showed evidence of these understandings, a final important component of the experience was the talk they had with working scientists.

Communication Between Students and Scientists. Another important feature of Passport projects is the way the Web is used to enhance links with the ongoing work of the scientists. These include Web postings of scientists' on-line field journals, and Web chats and e-mail exchanges between students and scientists. The following is an on-line journal entry from the project Web site posted by Jim Murphy, a meteorologist with Ames Research Center in California, and a member of the Pathfinder research team.

Students also had access to the professional and personal biographies of the scientists on the team.

FIELD JOURNAL FIELD JOURNAL

We Made It!
by Jim Murphy, Meteorologist
July 4, 1997

I'm sitting here at the Jet Propulsion Lab at 1:39 PM PDT, three and one half hours after Pathfinder successfully landed on Mars (which is just way cool to think about!!!), and I'm waiting for our first surface meteorology data, which we should receive in 26 minutes. This has been an absolutely terrific day for the spacecraft, and all of us who are interested in its success. The entry, descent, and landing apparently went just as designed (at least, that is the present indication), and we have a functioning spacecraft on the surface.[9]

Through journal entries such as these, students can keep pace with the scientific work, and identify with the scientists' triumphs and difficulties.

In addition, scheduled "Web chats" bring together classes of students from all over the country, and selected scientists who are ready to answer their questions about a given domain such as meteorology, rocketry, physics, etc. The following exchange shows the mix of personal, scientific, and speculative thinking that characterizes these conversations. This one is between Jim Murphy, and classes in Barre, Pennsylvania; Morris, Minnesota; Jenks, Oklahoma; and Sioux City, Iowa. Sandy, a "chat host" from NASA, helps moderate.

WebChat with Jim Murphy, Meteorologist

[Mrs. O's Class / Barre] Here's one of our questions for Jim. What's the difference in temperature between Mars and Earth?

[Jim Murphy / Ames 10:10:25]
In general, the temperatures on Mars are much colder than here on Earth. A warm day on Mars might have air temperatures near the ground get up to 40 degrees Fahren-

heit (but not very often or at too many places), while the coldest spots on Mars see temperatures as cold as −200 degrees Fahrenheit, which is colder than even the coldest temperature measured in Antarctica.

[Labbane Wood / Southeast Elementary]
Hello from Southeast Elementary in Jenks, Oklahoma! Sorry we're late . . . technical difficulties! We are fourth-graders in Mrs. Labbane's and Mrs. Wood's class. We're excited about chatting with you!

[Sandy / NASA Chat Host 10:12:49]
Welcome Labbane Wood Southeast Elem.!!! I'm very happy to see that you worked through your technical difficulties!!!

[Mrs O's Class / Barre]
Jim, how fast has the wind ever blown on Mars?

[Jim Murphy / Ames 10:26:09]
The wind on Mars has probably never blown faster than about 400 miles per hour. We can determine this because the wind can't blow faster than the speed of sound, and the speed of sound on Mars is 400 to 450 miles per hour; at the surface of Mars, I would guess that the fastest wind is probably 150 to 200 miles per hour . . . but that is really just a guess.

[Marske / Sioux Center Middle School]
Do you think we could ever live on Mars considering the weather there?

[Jim Murphy / Ames 10:12:57]
Yes, I think we could live on Mars even considering the temperatures there, but you would not catch me running around outside in shorts!! People who travel there will be required to live within contained environments (i.e. spaceships), since there is no air to breathe. Just as people now spend the winter at the Earth's South Pole (where it gets pretty darn cold), I think that we can deal with the cold Martian temperatures, especially if we were near the equator, where it probably does not get much colder than −120 degrees Fahrenheit or so. . . .

[Labbane Wood / Southeast Elementary]
Why isn't there an ozone layer on Mars?

[Jim Murphy / Ames 10:27:49]
Good question. There is essentially no ozone layer on Mars, since there is hardly any oxygen on Mars, and since to produce ozone the oxygen must be "broken" in half (producing two O molecules) with each molecule being added to another oxygen molecule. That lack of oxygen leads to a lack of ozone.

[Harris / 8th grade / KP North]
We have been studying weather and have been impressed with the differences in temp.—what are the temperature ranges now on Mars?

[Jim Murphy / Ames 10:15:00]
The maximum air temperatures near the surface are probably +40 Fahrenheit or so, while the coldest temperatures near the surface are probably −230 Fahrenheit or so.

[Mrs. Dabbs / 1st grade / WestView]
Are you worried about the weather harming the Pathfinder?

[Jim Murphy / Ames 10:30:01]
Well, I wish I were worried about the weather harming Pathfinder. We believe that Pathfinder is no longer working, probably because the cold temperatures cause some part of the inside of the spacecraft to break, since things tend to become more likely to break or crack when they get very cold (I always tend to think of plastic trash cans cracking in cold weather. . . .)[10]

Such exchanges as these begin to suggest what it means for students to "engage in discourse about science." What is notable in these exchanges is not that students necessarily understand all the science being talked about, but that they are asking questions of working scientists who treat those questions for what they are—serious expressions of curiosity worthy of a serious reply. In a way characteristic of adult talk about science, conversation shifts from the personal to the factual (what are the temperature ranges on Mars?) to the speculative (e.g., could we live on Mars, given the weather?). Students are learning that different kinds of reasoning are part of scientific inquiry.

Finally, it is worth noting that students' e-mail exchanges with scientists—their way of asking questions of individual experts at any time—are *facilitated* exchanges with *Passport*. Conversations between scientists and students do not happen naturally or easily; they have to be nurtured and facilitated. *Passport to Knowledge,* like other good projects linking students with the outside world, has protocols and supports for communication, including staff who signaled teachers about the need to translate between experts and novices. Again, from the research about the first year of implementation:

> Some of the postings from the scientist, Sanjay, were way above my younger students' level. I know that the program is aimed for the middle school, so I translate it when necessary. I have to translate most of the journals that are coming from the Pathfinder mission teams as well. About one third to a half of the kids would really get it. With the younger students, the activities and hands-on work from the guide were more flexible and easy to adapt for their use.
>
> —Fifth-grade teacher

In summary, it appears that the classrooms that actively participated in *Passport to Knowledge* activities had students producing work that demonstrated a more rigorous kind of science learning in keeping with new standards. Students' work was produced in classroom discourse, queries to experts, writing assignments, and projects as well as in diverse formats ranging from poetry to drawings and models to multimedia presentations.

Lest it be thought that the technologies were the driving forces in this success, it should be noted that two major barriers to teachers' and students' participation in *Passport* activities were, on the one hand, inadequate technology access, and more important, overly constraining curricula that teachers were obliged to "cover," leaving too little room to develop deep and meaningful project work like *Passport*. Changes in curriculum, in assessment, and in the organization of time and space for science learning, are thus all necessary for instructional change to occur with media-based projects like *Passport to Knowledge*.

Goal: Creating Communities of Science Learners

An important goal of the new science standards is creating communities of science learners who develop questions together, conduct research together, discuss their findings and what to make of them together, and share their work with a wide range of audiences. Creating community is not primarily a technological challenge, but technologies can help. In the following example, the Web serves primarily as a publishing medium for student work; students from around the world can thereby compare and discuss their findings as well as see their own thinking and expression validated in a public space.

The Wild Ones

The Wild Ones is an international club for students aged seven to fourteen, sponsored by the Wildlife Preservation Trust International. *The Wild Ones* Web site (http://www.thewildones.org) provides information about endangered species, different habitats, and environments. Guided by their teachers, students from all over the world create and publish most of the content of the Web site. Teachers and students may subscribe to become a member of the Club by using e-mail, fax, or snail mail. They may contribute their written work, artwork, photographs, and experiments.

The Web site hosts ongoing projects that classrooms can join, including an animal behavior study, bird feeder observations, a bird migration study, an environmental attitudes survey, environmental conditions monitoring, and habitat design. Each of these projects has a protocol that students follow in making and reporting their observations of animal life and local habitats. There are lesson plans to guide teachers and Web-based forms for submitting findings.

Significantly, *The Wild Ones* is interdisciplinary in spirit, encouraging students to use their imaginations in writing about and drawing the animals they are studying. As a result, students' writing and artwork is well represented in the published Web site. This personalizes the Web site and enables each student to see clearly his or her own contributions to the larger enterprise.

As a research resource, *The Wild Ones* site provides articles on endangered animals, each one describing the animal, its habits, habitat, threats to survival, and the work being done on the animal's behalf.

The Wild Ones Web site also contains e-mail contacts to scientists working in species and habitat preservation and restoration in the field. These specialists are arranged according to the animal or habitat they are expert in, and the scientists are prepared to respond to student questions.

Various on-line and print support materials are available to help teachers and students stay in touch with the project, including an on-line newspaper, *Wild Times,* and copies of *The Teacher Connection* for each registered teacher. Through foundation support, *The Wild Ones* is able to offer free subscriptions for up to fifty students and two teachers per school.

There is also a narrative device somewhat akin to *Carmen Sandiego* to hook students who need more hooking. Students can follow the adventures of Tammy Tamarin, *The Wild Ones* mascot who travels around the world to take part in adventures with members. Students can e-mail Tammy to invite her to join an adventure they are planning. Photographs and journal entries of these exploits will be published on *The Wild Ones* site.

Web image: Bank Street students in the zoo observing animals. (Photo by Michael Wilkinson, teacher.)

Web image: Students in the classroom discussing their animal observations.

In short, *The Wild Ones* aims to encourage and foster collaborative Internet projects. It coordinates student study of animal-related themes and publishes student work, including writing and artwork, it contains plenty of information about endangered species, and it allows students to contact specialists working in the field.

Sixth-grade students at the Bank Street School for Children in New York City have recently been studying environmental science in coordination with *The Wild Ones*. In their first project they charted environmental conditions in New York City over six weeks. When they posted their recordings on the Web (in standardized graphs representing temperature, precipitation, pH, humidity, and daylight), students were able to compare, for instance, their own environment's conditions with those posted by students in Bra, Italy. The surprisingly colder temperatures and lesser rainfall in Italy enabled students to speculate about the reasons for the disparity: season, latitude, elevation, ocean-borne weather patterns.

In their second activity, the Bank Street students began a long-term exploration of animal adaptations. Part of their work included trips to the Central Park Zoo to observe animals in the zoo's carefully created and naturalistic (if not natural) habitats. *The Wild Ones* Web page shows, through photos and text, the progress of their work. (Students took photographs of the animals themselves; the teacher photographed the process of student work.) First, students are seen at the zoo observing tamarins, monkeys, river otters, and penguins, drawing them, and making notes about their behaviors and their habitats. Next, students are seen back in the classroom, comparing and discussing their observations in small groups, trying to come to consensus about the ways their animal is adapted to its environment, and keeping track of questions or difficulties that emerge. Then students are seen at the computer, typing e-mail questions to *The Wild Ones* scientists who are experts on the animal they are studying.

Finally, students expressed what they had learned in the form of creative articles about their animals. Students used their imaginations in writing about and drawing their animal but were also asked to integrate what they had learned about the way their animal was adapted—through behavior or through bodily form—to its environment. The assignment (and perhaps the promise of Web publication) proved very motivating for students. Taking advantage of the class discussion of upcoming national elections, the teacher encouraged some students to write about "animal politics," prompting them to decide "which candidate will your animal vote for?" Here is a girl named Lea's response:

We Ask Them—Bill or Bob?
by Lea of the Bank Street School for Children, NYC
(Web graphic)

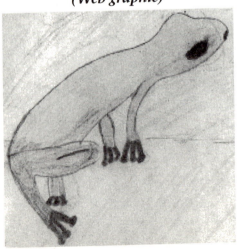

If the poison arrow frog was participating in the November presidential elections, it would vote for Bill Clinton. First of all, Clinton spends a lot of money on children's issues, such as health care. When the poison arrow frogs tadpoles are born, the male frog carries the babies on his back to keep them moist, and that's health care. That's one reason why the poison arrow frog would vote for him. He wouldn't vote for Bob Dole because he spends a lot of his money on defense, and the poison arrow frog only uses its defenses when it's in extreme danger.

Another reason that the poison arrow frog would vote for Clinton is that the poison arrow frog makes a chirping and buzzing sound to communicate with other frogs. Clinton is a very good communicator, but Dole isn't, because he tends to be boring.

Many of the student articles integrate detailed observations that students made at the zoo, as in the following entry by a girl named Anna:

Hyperactive Otters!
by Anna of the Bank Street School for Children, NYC
(Web graphic)

Anna, SFC

All throughout the day, otters never stop moving or playing with each other. This is absolutely hilarious! Some people say that the playing is a part of the close social structure of the otter. Others, like me, just think it's because they think very much like human children. While in the water, otters swim up to each other and jostle each other from above or below. I can never understand why the jostled otter never gets upset at the other one. Once, while observing them, I saw a male otter swim in and out of a sunken tree branch. He could be training for the water Olympics!

I think the reason for so much otter movement is that all river otters are hyperactive. Why else would otters run around a riverbank, jump into the water, and swim upstream all in one minute?

❖ A Note about Studying Nature at the Zoo

The use of a zoo as a context for students to learn about animals' adaptations to their environments must be pedagogically justified as a better choice than having students learn by observing local animals in their natural habitats. Obviously the zoo makes close observation easier for students, and it also makes available interesting animals not found locally. But it raises a host of important media literacy questions. Zoos, after all, are *representations* of nature; they are themselves highly constructed *media* that give us privileged access to animals but also contain and constrain both the animals' behavior and our own behavior as observers.

In this case, the teacher was focused on having students note general morphological features of organisms and their relationships to the environment—for example, the fact that tree frogs have suction feet that enable them to hold on to wet twigs and leaves, and that as relatively defenseless prey they are camouflaged green in order to hide from predators. At this level of analysis, which is appropriate to sixth-graders, it may not be important to discuss the zoo as a representational medium. But with older students, or where the focus is on animal *behavior* and not simply morphology, a host of questions should be raised about the zoo as a constructed artifact. For example: In what significant ways are the zoo habitats different from the animals' natural environments? How might these differences (including the presence of human observers) affect animal behavior? What does the zoo's design suggest about how its creators want us to relate to the animals? How do the different design elements—lighting, landscaping, architecture, air treatment, audio, exhibitry, and signage—all shape what we feel and think about the animals?

While playful and highly expressive, student work in *The Wild Ones* project can lead to just the kinds of science learning that new standards are calling for. Students like Anna used their minds to connect direct observations of the animals to larger generalities about animal behavior and finally raise questions that they attempt to answer through their own reasoning, citing evidence if they can. They leave, however, with a sense of the open-endedness about their topic: it is not a closed book, but an open one, with much more to learn about.

In this process the technology has played several key roles. First, it is a means of research, bringing together images and information about many animals that are not in books. Second, it is a tool for recording, sharing, and reflecting on data. For example, students used a camcorder and still camera to capture the behaviors and habitats of their animals, and also their fellow students. They used the standardized graphing forms to record and graph their environmental conditions data. The medium helped serve to bridge the school and nonschool worlds, in the e-mail interactions with scientists. Finally and most important, the Web was a publishing medium in this case, a way for students to share their work with real audiences and understand that their own thinking matters. Their personalized articles and artwork speak volumes about how engaged and how intellectually focused students were in the process.

Goal: Helping Students Learn from Advanced Representations of Scientific Phenomena

As the use of advanced technologies in the sciences has increased, so has the complexity of the representations of scientific and mathematical data that scientists use in their work. The ever-increasing power of computers coupled with advances in recording technologies and graphics have led to ever more subtle, dynamic, and complex portrayals of everything from the workings of the human body to the movement of weather patterns, from the behavior of microorganisms to the composition of planets and even stars. Scientists now record, analyze, and communicate about phenomena using these complex representations. Increasingly, they are available to nonscientists, through CD-ROMs, and especially, through the Web.

When high-performance networked computers first made it possible to deliver these kinds of data to students, educational technologists were excited. "Now students will be able to study phenomena using these resources, just like adult scientists do!" they said. Yet the use of these resources in elementary, middle, and secondary education raised a host of problems. Simply turning students loose on beautiful satellite imagery or microscopic photography led to utter confusion. What was ignored were the crucial differences between novice and advanced viewers of these materials. Novices, by definition, lack the background knowledge needed to interpret much advanced imagery, which is often highly coded. Hazarding the most basic interpretation of an infrared weather map, for example, requires that one understand that different colors represent different heat gradients, something few middle- or high-school students know without being told (and advanced representations, unlike textbooks, do not usually provide the contextualization, or "key," for you). In addition, students bring many misconceptions to visual materials, habits of observation and inference that are very different from those of trained adults.

These experiences led to a more explicit framing of the questions: What can relative novices gain from working with advanced visualizations? Is there a way to "scaffold" students' experience, starting from relatively simple and concrete imagery and moving to more complex representations? Can students' ability to interact with dynamic representations—for example, by manipulating animations, predicting what will happen, and then observing the outcome—help them think more complexly about phenomena that are difficult if not impossible to observe otherwise? What new kinds of skills do students need to learn from these visualizations, and what knowledge and skills do they gain?

A number of CD-ROM and Web projects suggest that complex visualizations can, if properly selected, framed, and contextualized with supporting materials help students inquire deeply into complex phenomena such as weather, planetary motions, anatomy, and microbiology. We shall look briefly at one exemplary use of complex visualizations for middle- and high-school students, Visualizing Earth.

Visualizing Earth

Visualizing Earth exploits the power of remote-sensing and geographic information systems (GIS) as tools for students to investigate our planet, to learn about the geosciences, and to develop skills of geographic visualization, problem solving, and investigative learning. The Visualizing Earth Web site (http://www.teaparty.terc.edu/ve/VisEarth-terc.html) serves as a gateway to many of the most powerful GIS displays. Most important, however, it contains carefully constructed educational activities that guide students through well-selected images toward the understanding of basic geoscience concepts and the practice of scientific thinking.

Among the notable features of the project are:

♦ inquiry around well-selected "anchor images" that are sequenced to yield key concepts;

♦ juxtaposition of imagery to provoke observation and critical thinking;

♦ use of still imagery and animations to encourage model building and prediction, then observation, and revision of hypotheses;

♦ widening of inquiry to embrace more complex visualizations on other sites;

♦ explicit consideration of the difference between expert and novice thinking about the visualizations.

The following outline for a series of introductory on-line activities around weather imagery illustrates some of these features.

EXPLORING IMAGES: WEATHER

Goals:

♦ Describe Earth as a dynamic and changing system, paying attention to relationships and interactions.

♦ Read, compare, interpret, and use visual information to extend understanding of Earth and its atmosphere.

Central Question:

♦ What are the relationships and connections among Earth's land, water, and atmosphere?

Investigations:

Investigation 1—Getting Oriented
The students are asked to study the Apollo 17 image without clouds and talk about what they see. They are then

given the Apollo 17 image with clouds and compare the two.

Investigation 2—Local View
Students generate the story for a pair of images that have been specifically selected to bring forward important concepts:

> Clouds over Oahu: influence of elevation
> Great Lakes: a midlatitude storm system
> Florida: convection

The students then "hear" the scientist's interpretation of the image pair and reconsider their own ideas. To set the stage for moving to the global view, each pair of images is set in a world context using the geosphere image.

Investigation 3—Global View
Students study the geosphere image and identify features, e.g., rivers, snow, mountains that can be seen. They then consider which of these might be indicators of weather and predict where clouds might be on the geosphere image.
    They compare their prediction to an image of global cloud cover and temperature, and then analyze an animation of cloud cover and temperature over a seven-day period.

Investigation 4–6—Local Views Revisited
Each of the three stories are extended and revised as more images and animations are studied.

Investigation 7—Culmination
Each student team is given a "mystery image" and asked to "uncover" its story.

The outline above is merely the first level of a multilevel Web that contains embedded links to still satellite imagery and animations, and step-by-step guidance in analyzing images and modeling one's own understanding of weather patterns and their relationships to land, water, and temperature. Yet the outline suggests many of the features that are significant in Visualizing Earth,

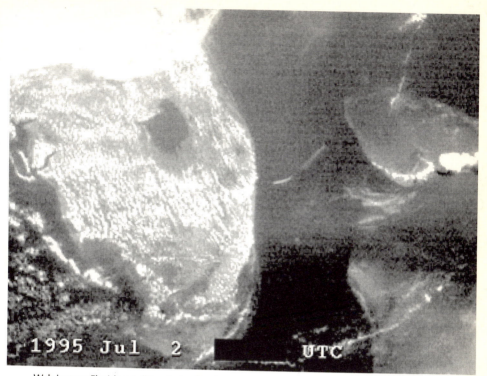

Web image: Florida satellite photo showing cloud cover. (Source: Visualizing Earth Web site http://www.teaparty.terc.edu/ve/VisEarth-terc.html)

and that make it a unique use of advanced visualizations for learning earth science. There is careful sequencing of materials in accordance with a notion of cognitive development and of pedagogy (going from introduction to culminating activity, from local images to global images, from basic concepts to their application); there are uses of animation to encourage students to observe, predict, and test weather patterns; and there are opportunities for students to build their own models and compare their thinking to that of scientists around the same images.

Perhaps most unusual, the Visualizing Earth Web site encourages teachers to consider the differences between students' and scientists' modes of interpreting global imagery such as satellite photos. For teachers to understand these differences is for them to have the initial tools to help scaffold student understanding in the right directions. Here, for example, are contrasting ways that young novices and adult experts look at satellite images of the earth:

Students	*Scientists*
A lot of clouds. A lot of blue sky too. It's Africa and that looks like the Middle East.	The first thing I notice is a view that is of the southern hemisphere portion of the earth.
This looks like some of the continents. Africa or something.	Now, the thing that strikes me immediately is that it's nearly all clear over the desert. There is practically nothing, no clouds or very little on the desert area. Now, we know that deserts are areas where the air is sinking, so you don't expect much clouds. So clouds form when the air rises. You cannot have any clouds forming when the air is actually sinking. So, the reason deserts are there is that the air is actually sinking. So there are no clouds, and it is dry.
People tell people all the time that there is more water than land, but it is just so hard to imagine because we are always walking on land.	
The white stuff looks like clouds and under it looks like part of a continent, pink stuff. It doesn't really look like a globe 'cause you can't really see all the continents and stuff 'cause the clouds are over them.	

Conclusion

Scientists tend to view the earth as systems instead of discrete parts. They see relationships between land, water, and atmosphere, and recognize seasonal and daily cycles. Students, on the other hand, tend to focus most attention on the land and often try to look through the cloud cover.

This kind of clarity about how novices think differently about complex data than do experts who are well trained in a discipline is all too rare when teachers begin to use scientific visualizations with their students. Teachers who attend to these differences are in a much better position to help students develop real understanding of scientific concepts by using these visualization tools.

Goal: Using Simulations of Complex Systems and Interactions to Help Students Develop and Test Their Own Concepts about Phenomena

An increasing emphasis on math and science standards is giving children opportunities for "tinkering and thinking"—setting up and observing interactions in a simple or complex system, and predicting and finding patterns in outcomes. Computer-based simulations of natural phenomena are important tools for helping students do this. Several genres of simulations support this kind of learning activity.

Microworlds

Microworlds are simulations of simple, idealized systems. Generally the goal in using microworlds is to develop facility with the basic interactions of variables operating in a system rather than to teach students about the way a real-world system works. The well-known population simulation *The Game of Life* falls into the microworld category. A very simple simulation of population change, *The Game of Life* enables students to set the initial conditions for a population of organisms and run time forward to see whether the organisms survive into the next generation, based on a very simple set of rules for birth, survival, and death. A Web-based version of this ubiquitous simulation is maintained by the University of Rochester in New York at http://barnyard.syr.edu/life.shtml.

There are, however, microworlds that do model real-world phenomena fairly closely. Gravity, friction, motion, and inertia are all physical phenomena that users can explore in *Thinking Things Three,* a CD-ROM "tool kit" of games and simulations that can provide compelling contexts for student tinkering and thinking about basic physics phenomena. *Thinking Things Three* is published by the software company Edmark.

Procedural Simulations

Procedural simulations model scientific procedures without the difficulty and mess that accompany students' performing the real-world version of the activity. Of course, like all simulations, they filter out important real-world information, and this should be discussed with students. Examples are *Sim Frog* and *A.D.A.M.*, CD-ROM–based simulations that enable students to study the anatomy of frogs and humans, respectively, without dissecting real organisms. One potential benefit of these simulations can be to allow students or parents who have religious or philosophical objections to dissection, or to frank scrutiny of the human body, to participate in learning activities they might otherwise miss or be uncomfortable about.

Published by Broderbund, *A.D.A.M.* allows students to dissect their way through over one hundred layers of anatomical illustrations of the human body, gives teachers a "fig leaf" option they can use to cover the model's genitals, and allows them to customize the race of the model. The use of these kinds of features in a simulation should raise many questions in the media literate classroom—for example about the meanings and values that people bring to scientific research using human and animal subjects.

Activity Simulations

Activity simulations are those that model science-related activities that occur in the real world: simulated expeditions to the rain forest to collect and classify plant and animal species; simulated geological digs that enable students to construct theories about geologic changes; a simulated research study in which kids follow along with scientists as they study the migration of monarch butterflies. As these examples suggest, the power of activity simulations is that they create a motivating, real-world context for scientific investigation, data gathering, and problem solving.

A CD-ROM called *Ecosystems: Island Survivors* shows how. Part of a larger package of software and videos that constitute *The Voyage of the Mimi* science and math curriculum, *Island Survivors* uses an ecology simulation to explore the concept of interdependency, covering topics such as energy, food webs, and populations. The program enables students to set up the initial conditions on an island ecosystem, then try to survive on the island (after they are "shipwrecked" there) by interacting among the plant and animal species. Students hunt, fish, and farm, and introduce various environmental stresses while monitoring the island species' population levels over a year. Survival for a year is difficult and usually takes multiple tries, as students refine their understanding of how the species interact, and how their own presence impacts upon them. The program, published by Sunburst Communications, is just one of many examples of activity simulations that, well used in the classroom, can provide a rich context for student thinking and problem solving.

Goal: Using Technologies as Tools to Support the Process of Data Collection, Analysis, and Presentation

A useful mantra for technology use in schools is "real tools for real purposes." Thoughtful educators strive to resist the frequently "dumbed down" and "kid-ified" educational software that exists in so many schools and instead seek educational uses of computers that reflect their important functions in the real, adult world. Word processing programs, spreadsheets, databases, e-mail, video recording, and the like have transformed the way business, science, government, and myriad other enterprises are conducted, yet only word processing has begun to penetrate schools.

It is important for students to use these real-world tools, but not for the reasons most often cited. Generally the rhetoric supporting students' use of tool technologies calls for "computer literacy," or "preparation for the high-tech workplace" of the twenty-first century. In truth, skills students develop with this or that particular software program will almost certainly be obsolete in the job market by the time students graduate. Students should indeed be familiar with a variety of technology applications and their uses, but this should not be an end in itself; it is something that can be accomplished en route to more important ends. As always, the more important end is for students to learn to use their minds well. Technology tools such as those above, when used in the context of inquiry and problem solving, can support exactly the same kinds of "tinkering and thinking" that simulations can.

The science teacher is in a unique position to make authentic use of technology tools in helping students develop deep understanding of science concepts, because the practice of science itself is steeped in the use of these tools. Among those that will be discussed here are MBLs and video recording technologies.

Microcomputer-based Laboratories (MBLs)

A key example of the tool use of computers in science is the microcomputer-based laboratory, or MBL, sometimes called CBL (for computer-based laboratory). The basic idea of an MBL is to transform the classroom computer into a powerful laboratory tool by attaching probes and sensors to it that enable students to measure and graph a variety of data. The importance of MBL is that it provides an excellent, highly interactive learning experience that removes much of the drudgery often associated with labs, and allows students to focus on the underlying science. There is some evidence to suggest that lectures, problem sets, or conventional labs, singly or in combination, are not as successful as well-constructed MBLs in conveying crucial scientific ideas such as mechanics concepts.[11]

Computer interface probes to measure light, sound, and temperature are now commonplace. Packages that involve measurement of pH, voltage, heart rate, skin resistance, ECG, EMG, optical absorption, earthquakes, visual illusions, response time, dissolved oxygen, force, magnetic field, pressure, turbidity, wind speed, insolation, heat flow, humidity, and much more are available. Battery-operated interfaces for field measurements are available as well. A large provider of MBL software and associated hardware packaged to meet the demands of middle school and high school science curricula in biology, physics, and other areas is Vernier Software, at http://www.vernier.com.

Video Recording and Display

Video is now a commonplace research tool in many fields, and especially the social and natural sciences. Video is most often used to capture time-based phenomena for in-depth study. Given that video can be slowed down, stopped, and played again, and that select frames can be used to illustrate stages in a linear process, it can serve as a powerful tool of observation and analysis. Considering how ubiquitous video camcorders are in schools, video could be used to advantage in science teaching and learning much more than it currently is.

Two brief examples follow. A class of sixth-graders studying animal behaviors decided that it had an interesting mystery right under its nose—the fish tank in the corner. Students decided they wanted to create a science fair presentation around the question Do fish sleep? The students noticed that the fish didn't appear to sleep during the day, and wondered if they slept at night. So they decided to use video as a way to find out. First, of course, they had to figure out a way to define what constituted sleep, since it was hard to tell just by looking. They came up with a definition based on whether the fishes' amount of movement in the tank decreased significantly. If it did, they were sleeping. Students set up the video camera in frame-capture mode, at intervals of ten seconds, and left for the day. Next day they had hundreds of snapshots of the fish in varying positions in the water. After exhaustively charting and analyzing them, they decided that the data did not argue in favor of fish sleeping.

A group of eighth-grade students preparing for the science fair in the same school was conducting an experiment on soil erosion. The problem was that after an hour and a half of preparing a model beach and preparing to flood it with waves, their experiment was over—and a mess as well—in only seconds. They decided to set up a video camera over the experiment to capture the different phases of the beach erosion under two different conditions. The video record enabled them to return to the data later many times for their analysis and enabled them to note features of the beach's changing shape that they might not otherwise have seen. For their science fair presentation, students scanned selected images into the computer and created an interactive slide show that parents and others could use to review the data they had collected, in succinct and colorful visual form. This left students free to be "explainers"—able to talk with parents about the substantive conclusions they had drawn, and why.

Goal: Understanding the History and Relations between Science, Technology, and Innovation

A final science learning goal we will address is students' need to understand the history and relationships between science, technology, and innovation. One new feature of the new science standards is a call for students to understand how science, technology, and society are interdependent, and for critical thinking about technology and invention to be infused in the science curriculum.

Positioning technology and innovation as a topic of investigation in the science classroom is not primarily an issue of using technology-based tools and materials but is rather a matter of asking certain questions and developing certain habits of mind. These are, in essence, media literacy habits of mind. Who has invented a technology, and for what social purposes? What form does the technology take, and who are the constituents who struggle to own and/or control it? Whose interests does its use at different times serve and not serve? These questions touch on the issues raised at the beginning of this chapter when we discussed the importance of science literacy in a world in which science and technology shape our lives—and therefore our history—in so many ways.

In the sciences, as in the humanities, point of view (meaning the perspective, both literally and figuratively, one has on one's object of study) plays a role in forming knowledge. Scientists have struggled to limit the role that point of view plays in their work and to achieve an unbiased, objective knowledge of their world; the scientific method was created to help them do so. But since Albert Einstein announced his theory of relativity, which suggested that the forces of the universe remain constant but man's observation of those forces changes with his changing conditions, many scientists have come to understand that the knowledge they create must take into account the context of that creation. For example, the knowledge gained from studying animals in a laboratory differs from the knowledge gained if those animals were studied in their natural habitat.

Just as scientists critically examine their own work for biases of any kind, teachers need to examine critically the media products they use to help students build their knowledge about the world. This applies to the content of textbooks and materials—teachers must make sure they are up-to-date with the rapid advances in knowledge—as well as the pedagogy of those materials: teachers must ensure that they incorporate improved teaching methods and are sensitive to the diverse audiences that will use them. For example, are the four food groups being taught or is the food pyramid introduced? Is the material based upon the lecture format or are students encouraged to experiment with the material? Does the material represent and address a particular audience—e.g., all white, of European descent, and male—or are other groups addressed and represented?

Moreover, just as scientists integrate a critical examination of their own and others' work into their research, you should integrate this critical activity into your curriculum as opposed to undertaking it as a separate area of study. Encouraging students to use their sources critically is part of the scientific method, part of examining the evidence, part of the process of situating the point of view used to gain knowledge and of understanding the context for that knowledge. Though students in the sixth to eighth grades are still heavily dependent on received knowledge in most aspects of their lives, they are beginning to question that knowledge and that dependence and should be encouraged to develop the means for a critical use of resources.

It is important to make students aware of the diverse history of technology to counteract the misleading stereotypes and assumptions about inventors, not only to teach the contributions to our daily lives that have come from all over the world but also to emphasize the profoundly social nature of invention. Perhaps the greatest misconception about invention is the notion of the inventor working alone in his laboratory. Any cursory examination of the history of invention will show that contributions to the tools, devices, machines, and procedures of mankind have come from all sources and that rarely have individuals working isolated from society helped to advance the technology of society.

One of the best Web resources available for helping students understand the embeddedness of science and technology in social practices is a project of the Smithsonian Institution's Lemelson Center for the Study of Invention and Innovation. It is titled *Whole Cloth: Discovering Science and Technology Through American Textile History* and is available at http://www.si.edu/lemelson/centerpieces/whole_cloth. The interdisciplinary project presents cutting-edge historical content in African American, women's, labor, and social history through interactive and document-based activities, all of which reveal how science and technology have been shaped by many different actors. It can help students learn that people such as themselves have always used and understood technology and have always been inventive. Students taught these lessons may be more likely to explore careers in technology and science, making the benefits of science more available to us all.

◆ Conclusion

In summary, we can say that based on our survey of science education principles and genres of new media, there are several key science-learning goals that media products can support:

- ◆ making complex scientific representations interactive and understandable;
- ◆ supporting students' thinking process by making phenomena observable, repeatable, and measurable;
- ◆ simulating complex systems and processes so that learners can engage in observation, prediction, and testing of their ideas about phenomena;
- ◆ promoting conversation and debate about science;
- ◆ helping students experience the connectedness of science to real-world settings, activities, and problems;
- ◆ modeling real-world uses of technology, not dumbed-down uses;
- ◆ connecting students who are underrepresented in science education and science careers with adult role models who can support them as learners.

◆ Annotated List of Science Web Sites

Science—General

The MAD Scientist Network
http://pharmdec.wustl.edu/YSP/MAD.SCI.html

The Mad Scientist Network is an interactive ''ask a scientist'' interface staffed by scientists actively engaged in science education and research at institutions around the world. Submit a question to be answered by members of the network.

Eisenhower National Clearinghouse Science
http://www.enc.org/ressci.htm

Good collection of science Web sites includes hotlists for chemistry, earth science, life science, museums and zoos, physics, and space science

The Observatorium
http://observe.ivv.nasa.gov/

NASA's public access site for earth and space data

What's New in the World of Science
http://www.exploratorium.edu/learning_studio/news/

The Exploratorium Learning Studio
http://www.exploratorium.edu/learning_studio/

Discover magazine
http://www.enews.com/magazines/discover/

Articles that reinforce fundamental topics and explain current events. Includes current issue, archives, information about their school science program, and more

An Inquirer's Guide to the Universe
http://www.fi.edu/planets/planets.html

The Weather Channel on the Web!
http://www.weather.com/weather/

Women of NASA: Web chat
http://quest.arc.nasa.gov/webchat/won-chat.html

Science Daily Magazine
http://www.sciencedaily.com/index.htm

Earth Science

The Nine Planets
http://www.seds.org/billa/tnp

Tour of the solar system with pictures, text, movies, and references to other WWW resources. Overview of the history, mythology, and current scientific knowledge of each of the planets and moons in our solar system

Franklin Institute Space Science Hotlist
http://sln.fi.edu/tfi/hotlists/space.html

Includes hotlists for the solar system, space travel/exploration, distant stars, background information, images, and teacher resources

Exploring Planets in the Classroom
http://www.soest.hawaii.edu/SPACEGRANT/class_acts/

Hands-on science activities are provided in classroom-ready pages for both teachers and students exploring geology, earth, and planetary sciences.

Volcano World
http://volcano.und.nodak.edu/

Everything volcanoes! A terrific Web site complete with download-able *HyperStudio* stack, lessons, and a great FAQ section

Blue Ice: Focus on Antarctica
http://www.usinternet.com.onlineclass

"Virtual" field trip to Antarctica, focus on the food web and geology/global warming. World experts are available by e-mail weekly, and the Web page is full of information and links to research sources around the world. Fee for participation

Earth and Sky
http://www.earthsky.com/

The award-winning *Earth and Sky* radio program presents natural science in a fun and easy-to-understand way. The Web site includes the daily show (transcripts, real audio, and links), searchable archives of past shows, and more.

Chemistry

WebElements
http://www.shef.ac.uk/~chem/web-elements/

This is an on-line periodic table that will be useful for those studying chemistry.

Chemistry Teacher Resources
http://rampages.onramp.net/~jaldr/chemtchr.html

This Web site, for chemistry teachers of grades nine through twelve, provides labs, information sheets, and other resources for teachers.

Paleontology

Diplodocus
http://www.iconos.com.toolsbone.html

Paleontology Without Walls
http://ucmpl.berkeley.edu/exhibits.html

Physics

Drivers, Start Your Engines!
http://www.lvjusd.k12.ca.us/EAMS_Science_Pages/
  IndyHunt.html

How science and technology play a part in developing stronger and safer cars by collecting data pertaining to the Indianapolis 500

Pilot to Physics
http://www.tp.umu.se/TIPTOP/

The Physics Classroom
http://www.glenbrook.k12.il.us/gbssci/phys/Class/BBoard.html

Newton's Apple Educational Materials
http://ericir.syr.edu/Projects/Newton/

Biology

Energy Flow in Amazonia
http://www.cccnet.com/success/energy_preview/
  energy_prev.html

How do plants, animals, and other organisms obtain the energy they need to live? What does an energy pyramid demonstrate about how energy is used in an ecosystem? The concepts of energy flow and food chains

Franklin Institute's Animals Hotlist
http://sln.fi.edu/tfi/hotlists/animals.html

A good selection of links including background resources, images, and teacher resources

Whale Songs
http://www.ot.com/whales/

Whale songs presented in conjunction with the International Fund for Animal Welfare's research vessel, *Song of the Whale*

Electronic Zoo
http://netvet.wustl.edu/e-zoo.htm

This well-organized site is a great resource for links to animal information (veterinary science, pets, etc.). Warning—SLOW loading (graphics intense!)

Worm World
http://www.nj.com/yucky/worm/

Animal and Ecosystem Related Links
http://www.cs.uidaho.edu/~connie/interests-wildlife.html

Links to sites on wildlife, wildlife habitats, ecosystems, domestic animals, and more

CELLS Alive
http://www.comet.chv.va.us/quill/

CELLS alive! is illustrated with videomicroscopy and animation that shows the cells of the immune system interacting with pathogens.

Cow's Eye Dissection
http://www.exploratorium.edu/learning_studio/cow_eye/

Cow's Eye Dissection is one of the most popular demonstrations at the Exploratorium.

Genetics Tutorial
http://morgan.rutgers.edu/

Ten units with Quicktime movies and sound explain the concepts of genetics.

Zooary
http://www.poly.edu/~duane/zoo.html

The Zooary has activities that apply fundamental concepts of biology, chemistry, environmental science, physical science, and ecology, educating students on environmental concerns and conservation.

Neuroscience for Kids
http://weber.u.washington.edu/~chudler/neurok.html

For elementary- and secondary-school students and teachers who would like to learn more about the nervous system.

The Yuckiest Site on the Internet
http://www.nj.com.yucky/

Introduces the world of insects to the general public in a friendly and unintimidating way and features Cockroach World.

Nova Odyssey of Life
http://www.pbs.org/wgbh/pages/nove/odessey/textindex.html

BugWatch
http://bugwatch.com/index.html

Photographic essay of various insect species

Interactive Frog Dissection
http://teach.virginia.edu/go/frog

Interactive Frog Dissection uses photographs and videos to teach this common lesson.

Birds of a Feather
http://www.mcn.org/ed/cur/liv/ind/birds/

See how a Mendocino teacher used Internet resources to help first- and second-graders learn about birds.

The Heart: A Virtual Exploration
http://sln.fi.edu/biosci/heart.html

Explore the heart. Discover the complexities of its development and structure. Follow the blood through blood vessels.

Virus Outbreaks
http://www.who.ch/outbreak/outbreak_home.html

Interactive Guide to Massachusetts Snakes
http://klaatu.oit.umass.edu:80/umext/snake/

An interactive snake database that will probably be useful for many parts of the northeastern United States. Includes snake history, mythology, and more

Sea World/Busch Gardens Homepage
http://www.bev.net/education/SeaWorld/homepage.html

Includes animal information, educational resources, and more

NOTES

1. American Association for the Advancement of Science (AAAS), *Benchmarks for Science Literacy* (New York: Oxford University Press, 1993), p. xi.
2. National Research Council. *National Science Education Standards.* (Washington, D.C.: National Academy Press, 1997).
3. Ibid.
4. AAAS, op. cit.

5. The CD-ROM Shop. Web page excerpt, 1997. http://198.53.145.135/home.html

6. Rhonda Toon, "A Class Act on the Net," *Business Week,* July 28, 1997.

7. Quote from teacher participant. From R. Spielvogel and J. Thompson *Passport to Knowledge Year Two Report.* Technical report. (New York: Center for Children and Technology, Education Development Center, 1997), p. 70.

8. Excerpt from teacher e-mail communication. From R. Spielvogel and J. Thompson *Passport to Knowledge Year Two Report.* Technical report. (New York: Center for Children and Technology, Education Development Center, 1997), p. 92.

9. J. Murphy. On-line journal entry. Passport to Knowledge Web Site: National Aeronautics and Space Administration. http://quest.arc.nasa.gov/mars/team/journals/murphy/02.html

10. National Aeronautics and Space Administration. December 10, 1997, Web chat archive with Jim Murphy. Passport to Knowledge Web Site. http://quest.arc.nasa.gov/mars/events/webchats/12-09jm97.html

11. Ronald K. Thornton and D. R. Sokoloff. "Learning Motion Concepts Using Real-Time Microcomputer-based Laboratory Tools." *American Journal of Physics,* 1990, 58(9): pp. 858–867.

Index

◆ Cornelia Brunner ◆

Dr. Brunner has been involved in the research, production, and teaching of educational technology in a variety of subject areas for thirty years. In addition to conducting research projects about the relationship between learning, teaching, and technology, she has designed and implemented educational materials incorporating technologies to support inquiry-based learning and teaching in science, social studies, media literacy, and the arts. She has worked extensively with staff and students in a variety of school environments on curriculum development projects, teacher support and training, and informal education. She has taught experimental courses at Bank Street College and the Media Workshop New York, in which teachers are introduced to new technologies, learn how to integrate technology into their curriculum, and learn how to use multimedia authoring tools to design their own educational programs. Dr. Brunner has also been an industry consultant for the design of educational and entertainment products for children of all ages during the last thirty years.

◆ Bill Tally ◆

Bill Tally is Senior Research Associate at the EDC Center for Children and Technology in New York City, a group of researchers and designers exploring the key roles technologies can play in educational change, toward more learner-centered, democratic schooling. With CCT he has studied young people's use of multimedia and network technologies in schools and community settings, has organized professional development for teachers to help them integrate technologies into their teaching, and has designed electronic materials for schools, museums, and public spaces. He holds a B.A. in psychology from the University of California at Santa Cruz, an M.A. in liberal studies from the Graduate Faculty of the New School for Social Research, and is currently a Ph.D. candidate in sociology at the City University of New York. He is a frequent speaker and writer on issues of education and media in electronic and print publications.

/